The Alberta Ballet Company
Presents

Repas de Deux

A cookbook for everyone
from the company
and their friends

coordinated and compiled
by
Caroline de L. Davies

Repas de Deux
by Caroline de L. Davies

First printing — April, 1985

Copyright © 1985 by
Caroline de L. Davies
6439 Silver Springs Way
Calgary, Alberta, Canada T3B 3G1

Canadian Cataloguing in Publication Data

Main entry under title:

Repas de deux

Includes index.
ISBN 0-919845-24-X

1. Cookery. 2. Ballet dancers — Alberta.
I. Davies, Caroline de L. II. Alberta Ballet
Company.
TX715.R46 1985   641.5   C85-091152-4

Photography by:
Peter Bolli
Bolli & Hutchinson Photographic Design Ltd.
Calgary, Alberta
Front cover photograph by:
Ross Hutchinson
Dishes and Accessories from:
Glass Haus (Calgary) Ltd.
Mount Royal Village, Calgary
Guenthers' Mobilia — Furniture and Accessories
524 - 17th Avenue S.W., Calgary
Village Cuisine
Mount Royal Village, Calgary
Supplies and testing by:
Maple Leaf Mills, Toronto

Design by Blair Fraser
Designed, Printed, and Produced in Canada by
Centax of Canada
1048 Fleury Street
Regina, Saskatchewan, Canada   S4N 4W8

#105 - 4711 13 Street N.E.
Calgary, Alberta, Canada   T2E 6M3

For many years I have been associated with the Alberta Ballet Company and have had the opportunity to watch its growth and development to its present success and artistic maturity. I was therefore delighted to be asked to contribute to "Repas de Deux".

The proceeds from the sale of this cookbook will be totally devoted to the future development of the Alberta Ballet Company. Your purchase will not only enrich your culinary library but in a very tangible way contribute to the continued success of the company and its dancers.

It would be impossible to thank all those people who have contributed their expertise, time, energy and of course, their fabulous recipes to the formation of "Repas de Deux". However, to each and everyone of you who acquires this book, a very special thank you for your valuable support.

Bon Appetit!

Jeanne Lougheed

Jeanne E. Lougheed

Author's Note:

Like many people I enjoy collecting recipe books, and for a long time have thought about writing one to raise money for the Alberta Ballet Company. Little did I realize how much time such a project would take, nor that the mere mention of "recipe testing" would reduce my family to a series of moans and groans after the first month.

There were some amusing incidents though, such as the bran muffins that failed to rise no matter what the testers did to them. Comments on the evaluation sheets such as "probably would be dynamite for constipation sufferers" said it all. I decided not to include that recipe in the collection.

Another recipe which shall remain nameless tasted so bad that my husband labelled it with a skull and crossbones, along with advice on what to do if accidentally consumed by humans.

Fortunately most of the recipes which have been sent to me are delicious and I feel confident that many of them will become your personal favorites too.

I would like to thank the following people:

<u>Brian Bender</u> for donating so much time to draw the portraits included in this book.

<u>Brydon Paige,</u> artistic director of the Alberta Ballet Company, who used his contacts in the world of dance to obtain recipes from some very distinguished people indeed.

<u>Sandra Currie and David MacGillivray,</u> dancers with the Alberta Ballet Company, for their time and talent in posing for the front cover.

<u>Michael Hamer,</u> who after a few false starts, such as "Swan Lake on Toast", came up with the title of this book.

<u>My husband,</u> who retained both his sanity and his waist-line despite eating up to four suppers a night.

<u>Peter Bolli and his partner Hutch,</u> who were such perfectionists it took them an average of four hours to take each one of the wonderful photographs illustrating this book.

<u>All those of my friends</u> who have helped with the laborious process of recipe testing, particularly Coral Luscombe, without whose help I would still be in the kitchen.

<u>A special thank you</u> to Liz McKale and Blair Odney for all the extra work I have inflicted upon them.

<u>Everyone</u> who has contributed a recipe to this book. Some are famous, most are not. I thank them all equally.

<u>Lastly, a special thanks to</u> Margo Embury of Centax (the printers) for support and encouragement far above the call of duty.

Caroline de L. Davies

4

Table of Contents

Panamá
13ᵉ April. 1984

Dear Mr Davies,

It has been one of my life-long ambitions, now I fear never to be realised, that I would somehow become a good cook.

Long ago I could go as far as to roast a good piece of Scotch beef but now I doubt that I could make a piece of toast without burning it. So what contribution can I make to a cook-book?

Here in Panama, where the coconuts are hanging on the palm trees right outside our windows, they grate the fresh coconut and cook it with rice using

6

the coconut milk instead of water - it is excellent. The custom is to purposely allow some to stick to the bottom of the pan so that it gets

browned and crunchy; and they say it is always best when it warmed up the next day. Maybe its not everyones idea of food for ballerinas! Well, Taglioni's favourite dish was English plum pudding and Pavlova said she liked the English fruit pies - which are not light at all, at least not the good home-made ones.

I wish the book the greatest success and hope my failure will not mar it - I very truly Margot Fonteyn

Dame Margot Fonteyn

Dame Margot Fonteyn

Dame Margot Fonteyn was born in Reigate, Surrey, England.

As a child she studied ballet with Grace Bosustow and Nicholas Legat before moving to Shanghai in 1930. There she worked with George Goncharov. Returning to London, she entered the Sadler's Wells Ballet School, where she studied with Ninette de Valois, the Director, and Ursula Moreton.

Except for her frequent guest appearances and tours, Fonteyn has spent her entire career with the (English) Royal Ballet and its predecessors the Vic-Wells Ballet and the Sadler's Wells Ballet.

She made her Vic-Wells debut as a "Snowflake" in the 1934 production of Nutcracker. Fonteyn joined the newly formed Royal Ballet as a permanent guest artist in 1959.

She became Rudolf Nureyev's partner after his emigration from the Soviet Union in 1962.

Fonteyn was made a Dame of the British Empire in 1959 for her service to the above mentioned companies and the Royal Academy of Dancing, of which she has been president since 1954.

She is considered by many to be the finest technician of the mid and late twentieth century.

Appetizers
&
Hors D'Oeuvres

Larry Hayden's Pâté

1 lb. (500 g) chicken livers cut in
    half
¼ lb. (125 g) mushrooms,
    chopped
¼ cup (50 mL) finely chopped
    parsley
¼ cup (50 mL) finely chopped
    green onions
½ tsp. (2 mL) salt
½ tsp. (2 mL) thyme
2 tbsp. (25 mL) of brandy
½ cup (125 mL) dry red wine
¾ lb. (365 g) butter

Melt ¼ lb. (115 g) butter over medium heat in a skillet. Add livers, mushrooms, parsley, onions, salt and thyme. Cook, stirring frequently, until livers are still pink in the centre. Heat brandy in a small saucepan over high heat and set aflame. Pour over livers at once and shake skillet until flames die. Add red wine, cool to room temperature. Purée livers and liquid in blender until smooth, leave running and add ½ lb. (250 g) butter, cut into pieces, one at a time. Pour into a pan or mold. Cover and chill overnight. Unmold to serve. Garnish with parsley and pimientos. Serve with Melba toast, French bread or crackers. Serves 8-10.

Betty Farrally
Founder
Royal Winnipeg Ballet

Betty Farrally

Born in Bradford, England, Farrally was trained at the Torren School of Dance in Leeds. In 1938 she and Gwyneth Lloyd emigrated together to Canada where they co-founded a school which subsequently became the Royal Winnipeg Ballet Company.

Although they served as co-artistic directors until the late fifties, Farrally was always most involved in maintaining the high technical standards of the company and school, serving as ballet master rather than choreographer-in-residence.

Farrally now lives in B.C. but continues to teach and adjudicate across Canada. She has received the Order of Canada for her services to the world of dance.

Liver Paté

Thomas Walker

Born in Lethbridge, Alberta, Walker began his formal training with Miss Lois Smith in 1980. He also studied at the Joffrey Ballet School and the National Ballet School. After graduating with honours, he danced with Dansepartout in Quebec City, and spent a year with the Indianapolis Ballet Theatre.

He has studied under Glen Gilmore, Daniel Sellier, Choo Sang Goh, Alexandra Danilova as well as Laura Alonso from the National Ballet of Cuba.

½ lb. (250 g) butter
1 lb. (500 g) chicken livers
1-3 (1-3) cloves fresh garlic
     small sprig of fresh rosemary or thyme
3-4 (3-4) scallions
4 oz. (125 g) cream cheese

Melt the butter in a large covered skillet and gently cook the chicken livers, garlic, rosemary or thyme and the scallions, until the liver is cooked. Remove the lid and cook for an additional 5 minutes. Put the liver in a blender along with the other ingredients and purée. Add the cheese in small amounts while blender is still running, making sure that it is well blended into the liver mixture. Place in a serving dish and chill.

Serve with crackers or melba toast.
Serves 8-10.

Thomas Walker
Dancer
Alberta Ballet Company

Salmon Mousse

1 tbsp. (7 g) envelope unflavored gelatin
¼ cup (50 mL) cold water
½ cup (125 mL) boiling water
½ cup (125 mL) Hellmann's mayonnaise
1 tbsp. (15 mL) lemon juice
1 tbsp. (15 mL) finely grated onion
dash of Tabasco
¼ tsp. (1 mL) sweet paprika
1 tsp. (5 mL) salt
2 tbsp. (30 mL) finely chopped fresh dill, or ½-1
tbsp. (7-15 mL). dried dill, according to taste
2 cups (500 mL) finely flaked poached fresh
salmon
1 cup (250 mL) heavy cream

Soften the gelatin in the cold water in a large mixing bowl. Stir in the boiling water and whisk the mixture slowly until gelatin dissolves. Cool to room temperature.

Whisk in the mayonnaise, lemon juice, grated onion, Tabasco paprika, salt and dill. Stir to blend completely and refrigerate for about 20 minutes, or until the mixture begins to thicken slightly.

Fold in the finely flaked salmon. In a separate bowl, whip the cream until it is thickened to peaks and fluffy. Fold gently into salmon mixture.

Transfer the mixture into a 6 to 8 cup (1.5 - 2 L) bowl or decorative mold. Cover and chill for at least 4 hours.

Serve on toast, black bread or crackers, or serve as a first course garnished with watercress.
Serves 12.

Mrs. Jeanne Lougheed
Patron
Alberta Ballet Company

Mom's Crabmeat Spread

12 oz. (340 g) softened cream cheese
2 tbsp. (25 mL) Worcestershire sauce
2 tbsp. (25 mL) mayonnaise
1 tsp. (5 mL) lemon juice
1 (1) small onion — grated
½-¾ cup (125-175 mL) cup Heinz chili sauce
5½ oz. (156 mL) can crab meat flakes
parsley flakes

Mix first 5 ingredients. Spread on a serving dish in a layer ½"
(1 cm) thick. Spread chili sauce over this (as if icing). *DO NOT
MIX!*

Sprinkle on drained and rinsed crab meat. Top with parsley
flakes. Chill and serve with assorted crackers.

Serves 6-8

Nancy Shainberg
Former Principal Dancer
Alberta Ballet Company

See photograph page 16.

Cheese Pesto Mold

Base

> **1 lb. (500 g) unsalted butter**
> **1 lb. (500 g) cream cheese**

Filling: Pesto Sauce

> **½ cup (125 mL) butter**
> **½ cup (125 mL) freshly grated Parmesan cheese**
> **½ cup (125 mL) finely chopped parsley**
> **1 (1) clove garlic, crushed**
> **1 tsp. (5 mL) dried basil leaves**
> **½ tsp. (2 mL) dried marjoram leaves**
> **2 tbsp. (25 mL) olive oil**

Whip together the base ingredients with electric mixer until fluffy.

Blend all the filling ingredients except oil, in a bowl with a spoon or with a pestle and mortar. Gradually add olive oil to the mixture, beating constantly.

Wet a piece of cheesecloth and wring out. Drape inside a small straight-sided bowl (small soufflé dish works well). Cheesecloth must be large enough to hang down over the sides of bowl.

Put ¼ of the base mixture in the bowl and spread evenly with a spatula. Then put ⅓ of the pesto sauce over the base and spread evenly. Continue to layer ending with base mixture. Fold the ends of the cheesecloth over the mixture and press down to distribute the mixture evenly in the bowl.

Refrigerate for about an hour, until firm, and unmold, *removing cheesecloth*.

DO NOT LEAVE IN CHEESECLOTH. Store in Saran wrap in refrigerator.

Serve with crackers as an hors d'oeuvre.

Serves 14-16.

Sharon Mook

Cream Cheese Dip

1 (1) small onion, finely ground
½ lb. (250 g) softened butter
2 x 8 oz. (2 x 250 g) packages cream cheese,
    softened
    salt, pepper and garlic to taste
⅓ cup (75 mL) beer
1 (1) large loaf of brown or black bread

Blend first 6 ingredients. Add beer and mix well just before serving.

Hollow out a large loaf of heavy brown or black bread (rye, pumpernickle etc.) Reserve what is hollowed out for dipping. Pour mixture into loaf and serve with assorted vegetables and crackers in addition to the bread cubes.

Serves 16-20.

Heather Baker
President
Alberta Ballet Guild, Calgary

See photograph page 16.

Avocado Dip

2-4 (2-4) **avocados, mashed**
1 tbsp. (15 mL) vinegar
½ (½) **medium-sized onion, to**
    taste
1 (1) **clove garlic, crushed**
    juice of 1 (1) **lemon**
    a few drops of Tabasco sauce
    salt & pepper to taste
4 oz. (250 g) cream cheese

Put all the ingredients into the blender, and process until smooth. Serve with taco chips.
This avocado dip can be frozen.
Serves 8-12.

Marquita Lester
Ballet Mistress
Alberta Ballet Company

Marquita Lester

Marquita attended the National Ballet School in Toronto. She received numerous scholarships, including one of the first Canada Council Scholarships.

She danced with the National Ballet Company under the direction of Celia Franca, and left the company to co-found and direct the Lester School of Dance and the Trent Regional Ballet Association in Peterborough, Ontario from 1971 - 1981.

Ms. Lester was Ballet Mistress with the Calgary Dance workshop and the Calgary City Ballet Company. In 1983 she accepted the appointment of Ballet Mistress to the Alberta Ballet Company. She is also a faculty member with the professional dance program at the Banff School of Fine Arts.

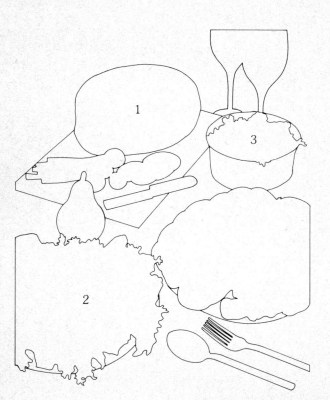

Marinated Shrimp

Suzanne Farrell

Born in Cincinnati, Ohio, Farrell trained at the Cincinnati Conservatory of Music. She was one of the first Ford Foundation scholars to the School of American Ballet to be accepted into the parent company, the New York City Ballet. Balanchine created "Tzigane" (1975) and revived "Chacone" (1976) for her and her partner, Peter Martins, and Jerome Robbins choreographed "In G Major" (1975) and the Central Pas De Deux "The Four Seasons" (1979) around them.

1 lb. (500 g) shrimp
6 tbsp. (90 mL) olive or vegetable oil
6 tbsp. (90 mL) lemon juice
⅓ cup (75 mL) tarragon vinegar
1 clove (1) garlic, crushed
1 tsp. (5 mL) salt
1 (1) bay leaf
2 tsp. (10 mL) sugar, optional
2 tbsp. (25 mL) chopped parsley
¼ tsp. (1 mL) pepper

Cook and devein shrimp. In a small saucepan, combine oil, lemon juice, vinegar, garlic, salt, bay leaf and sugar. Bring to boil. Pour over shrimp, add parsley and pepper. Toss lightly. Place in refrigerator to marinate. May be marinated for 2-3 days for extra flavor. Serve with thinly sliced brown bread and butter or assorted crackers.

*As a bonus, add sliced stuffed green olives! Serves 4.

Suzanne Farrell
Principal Dancer
New York City Ballet

Oyster Appetizer

3 **(3) dozen medium-sized oysters**
¾ cup (175 mL) chili sauce
2 tbsp. (25 mL) chopped green pepper
2 tbsp. (25 mL) Worcestershire sauce
10 (10) slices bacon, diced
¾ cup (175 mL) grated Parmesan cheese

Place the drained oysters in skillet. Cover with chili sauce, Worcestershire sauce and green pepper. Place in oven at 350°F (180°C) until oysters begin to puff. Sprinkle with bacon and cheese. Bake for a further 10 minutes.

Serve on dark rye bread.
Serves 6-10.

Charlotte Williams
Alberta Ballet Guild, Calgary

Brie en Croûte

A marvellous appetizer for large cocktail parties and buffet suppers

2 x 11 oz. packages (2 x 300 g) piecrust mix
5 lb. (2.5 kg) wheel of brie
2 (2) egg yolks
2 tbsp. (25 mL) water

Make up the pastry as directed on the package. Roll out half the amount to an 18" (45 cm) circle. Place on a large baking tray. Leaving outer crust of brie intact (remove paper), place cheese in the centre of the pastry round. Bring pastry up over cheese about 1" (2.5 cm) over edge. Press to make smooth all around.

Combine egg yolks with water. Brush a little over pastry rim on top of cheese. Roll ¾ of the second amount of pastry to form a 14" (35 cm) circle. Trim evenly to make 13" (32 cm). Place on top of brie, overlapping pastry edge.

Press with fingers to make a *tight seal.* Make decorative leaves with pastry trimmings. Arrange over top of brie. Brush with egg yolk mixture and refrigerate.

Two hours before serving bake in a 400°F (200°C) oven for 20 minutes. Brush again with egg yolk mixture. Bake 20-25 minutes longer until golden brown. Remove to wire rack. Let cool for about 1 hour. Remove to serving tray. Serve while *still warm.* Cut into thin wedges.

Left-overs may be reheated at 350°F (180°C) for 20 minutes. Serves 40.

Shelagh Aizlewood
Founder Member
Alberta Ballet Guild, Calgary

Pears in Tarragon Cream Dressing

>   2 (2) eggs
> 2½ tbsp. (35 mL) sugar
>   3 tbsp. (45 mL) tarragon vinegar
>   ½ cup (125 mL) whipping cream
>   ½ tsp. (2 mL) salt
>   ¼ tsp. (1 mL) pepper
> 3-4 (3-4) pears (tinned can be used if fresh ripe
>   pears are unavailable)
>   lettuce or cress
>   paprika

Beat eggs and sugar and gradually add vinegar. Stand in boiling water and stir until mixture begins to thicken. Stir until cooling. Leave until cold. Whip cream lightly and fold into dressing. Season with salt and pepper to taste. Peel pears, halve and remove cores and fibrous threads. Place lettuce on individual plates. Put pear half in centre, rounded side up. Coat each pear with dressing and shake a little paprika over the top. Serve one pear half per person. Serves 6-8.

Caroline de L. Davies
Member of Board of Directors
Alberta Ballet Company

See photograph page 16.

Deep-Fried Pears with Roquefort Butter

A scrumptious hors d'oeuvre — very rich and filling.

Pears

4 (4) Anjou pears
½ tsp. (2 mL) ginger
1 cup (250 mL) finely ground bread crumbs
1 egg, slightly beaten
¼ cup (50 mL) milk

Halve, core and peel pears. Dry thoroughly.
Combine the ginger and bread crumbs.
Mix egg and milk in a bow, dip pears in the "wash", then in the bread crumb mixture.
Deep-fry at 375°F (180°C) until golden brown — 3 to 4 minutes.
Cool. Place pears on bed of lettuce leaves and pipe Roquefort Butter into pear cavities.

Roquefort Butter

½ cup (125 mL) butter
3 oz. (80 g) Roquefort cheese
¼ tsp. (1 mL) Worcestershire sauce

Cream together well. Chill only slightly.

Raclette Restaurant
Toronto

Spanakotiropita

A traditional Greek spinach & cheese pie.

2 **lbs. (1 kg) spinach**
1 **cup (250 mL) chopped spring**
    onions
5 **eggs (5) beaten**
1 **lb. (500 g) feta cheese**
½ **cup (125 mL) chopped parsley**
1 **tbsp. (15 mL) chopped dried**
    dill
1 **lb. (500 g) phyllo pastry**
    salt and freshly ground black
    pepper, to taste
½ **cup (125 mL) melted butter,**
    approximately

Chop spinach, using leaves only, with onions. Steam until soft. Add cheese, eggs, dill and parsley, combine and mix well. Season with salt and pepper to taste.

Melt butter in a saucepan. Butter a 17½" x 12½" x 2" (45 cm x 30 cm x 5 cm) glass baking dish. Place 8-10 sheets of phyllo in the pan, buttering each with the melted butter.

Spread the filling evenly over the phyllo. Cover with another 10 sheets, brushing each 1 with the melted butter as before. Brush the top sheet and bake at 350°F (180°) for 1 hour. Cut into small squares or triangles to serve.
Serves 16-20.

Frank Augustyn
Principal Dancer
The National Ballet of Canada

Frank Augustyn

Born in Hamilton, Ontario, he entered the National Ballet School at the age of 12, and joined the National Ballet in 1970, becoming a soloist in 1971 and a principal in 1972. He rapidly took on most of the major roles in the repertoire.

Augustyn's many guest appearances include the Soviet Union, Germany, Italy, the U.S.A., Cuba, and Monte Carlo.

Augustyn has been described by William Littler of the Toronto Star as able to "infuse classical movement with dramatic meaning without sacrificing beauty of line."

In 1979 Augustyn was invested as an Officer of the Order of Canada and received an Honorary Degree from York University.

Mushroom Lover's Pie

Veronica Tennant

Tennant was born in London, England and trained at the National Ballet School. Joining the National Ballet in 1965 she was the youngest principal in the company. She soon established an international reputation in two award-winning films. In 1973 she danced Aurora opposite Rudolf Nureyev and in 1974, with Mikhail Baryshnikov in his first performance in the West.

As a guest artist Tennant has danced in Europe, North and South America, and Japan. Tennant was invested as an Officer of the Order of Canada in 1975 and is the author of a children's novel, "On Stage, Please". She has also been the subject of a CBC-TV documentary entitled "Veronica Tennant: A Dancer of Distinction", aired in February 1983.

This is a recipe that I created for my husband's surprise birthday dinner and it was a great success.

> 1 lb. (500 g) mushrooms, very thinly sliced
> ½ cup (125 mL) whipping cream, scalded
> 4 (4) eggs, well beaten
> ¾ cup (175 mL) grated Edam cheese
> 1 tsp. (5 mL) salt
> ¼ tsp. (1 mL) pepper
> ¼ tsp. (1 mL) nutmeg
> ¼ tsp. (1 mL) garlic powder (optional)
> 2 tbsp. (25 mL) finely minced parsley
> ¼ cup (50 mL) grated Parmesan cheese

Combine all ingredients, except for Parmesan cheese, and put in well-buttered quiche pan, pie plate or individual ramekins. Set in pan of hot water and bake in a 325°F (160°C) oven for 45-60 minutes. When well set, sprinkle with Parmesan cheese and run under broiler for 10 seconds.

Serve with garlic bread and a crisp green salad for lunch or with melba toast as an hors d'oeuvre. Serves 4.

Veronica Tennant
Principal Dancer
The National Ballet of Canada

Yakitori

Japanese-style broiled chicken brochettes.

Sauce

⅔ **cup (150 mL) soy sauce**
½ **cup (125 mL) sugar**
⅓ **cup (75 mL) sake or dry sherry**
½" **peeled fresh ginger root, cut into paper thin**
    slices (optional)

1 **lb. (500 g) boned chicken meat, or chicken**
    liver halves
2 **(2) scallions**
  bamboo skewers

In a saucepan combine soy sauce, sugar, sake and ginger. Boil until reduced to about ⅔ of original volume.

Cut chicken meat into bite-sized pieces. Cut scallions into 1" pieces. Skewer chicken meat, alternating with scallions.

If using chicken livers, first marinate in sauce for 3 to 4 hours, then alternate liver and scallion pieces on bamboo skewers.

Dip chicken/scallion skewers into sauce and place under pre-heated broiler or grill. Broil 1 side for 2 to 3 minutes, dip again into sauce and broil. Repeat 2 to 3 times. With chicken livers broil for 4 to 5 minutes each side.

If backyard cooking, use barbecue or hibachi as grill.
Serves 6-8.

Dr. H. J. Shimizu
Member of Board of Directors
Alberta Ballet Company

Soups
&
Breads

Chilled Cucumber Soup

Delicious for a summer luncheon with a salad.

**3 (3) English cucumbers, peeled, very finely
    chopped
8 oz. (250 g) plain yogurt (Yoplain)
3 cups (750 mL) milk
3 cups (750 mL) half and half cream
⅛ tsp. (0.5 mL) nutmeg
    white pepper
    salt
⅛ tsp. (0.5 mL) ginger
    shredded coconut**

Combine all ingredients, except coconut, adding extra spices to taste. Sprinkle coconut over the top. Serve chilled.
Serves 6-8.

Shelagh Aizlewood

Gazpacho

A refreshing soup for a hot summer evening.

1 cup (250 mL) tomato juice
½ cup (125 mL) iced water
6 tbsp. (75 mL) olive oil
2-3 tbsp. (30-45 mL) lemon juice
½ (½) clove garlic
2 lbs. (1 kg) ripe tomatoes, peeled, seeded and coarsley chopped
1 (1) cucumber, peeled and coarsely chopped
½ (½) Spanish onion, chopped
salt
freshly ground pepper
cayenne pepper

Garnish

½ (½) green pepper, diced
4 (4) slices white bread, diced and sautéed until crisp and golden in butter and olive oil
1 (1) avocado pear, peeled, stoned, diced and brushed with lemon juice to preserve color
4 tbsp. (50 mL) coarsely chopped parsley

Combine tomato juice, iced water, olive oil and lemon juice in a large soup tureen or serving bowl which has been rubbed with garlic. Add peeled, seeded and chopped tomatoes, including all the juice, the peeled and chopped cucumber and onion and generous amounts of salt, freshly ground black pepper and cayenne to taste. Chill thoroughly.

To serve, garnish each bowl with diced green pepper, fried croutons, diced avocados and chopped parsley.
Serves 4.

Shelagh Aizlewood

Stilton and Onion Soup

⅓ cup (75 mL) butter
1 (1) Spanish onion, thinly sliced
6 oz. (170 g) Stilton cheese, crumbled
⅓ cup (75 mL) flour
4 cups (1 L) chicken broth
1 (1) bay leaf
   salt and pepper to taste
½ cup (125 mL) whipping cream

Melt butter and sauté the onion until soft. Add cheese and stir until it has melted. Add flour and cook, stirring continuously, for 5 minutes.

Add chicken stock, bay leaf and seasoning. Bring to the boil and then simmer for 20 minutes. Remove the bay leaf. Add cream and serve with crusty bread and butter.
Serves 4.

Ann Black
Vice-President
Alberta Ballet Guild, Calgary

Cream of Stilton Soup

A rich and flavorful variation of the traditional vichyssoise.

2 lb. (1kg) leeks
1 lb. (500 g) potatoes
4 tbsp. (50 mL) butter
1 (1) stalk celery, thinly sliced
2½ cups (625 mL) chicken stock
2½ cups (625 mL) milk
   salt & black pepper to taste
1¼ cups (300 mL) whipping cream
⅛ tsp. (0.5 mL) nutmeg
3 - 4 oz. (75-125 g) Stilton per person

Prepare the vegetables. Slice the white of the leeks into ¼" diagonal pieces.

Dice the potatoes.

Melt the butter in a 2-quart (2 L) saucepan. Add the leeks and potatoes. Cook for 7 minutes, stirring continuously. Add celery to pan. Pour in the stock and milk and bring slowly to the boil. Add the seasonings to taste.

Simmer for 25 minutes or until the vegetables are tender. Allow the soup to cool. Purée the mixture in a blender or food processor. Before serving, gently heat the soup; add the crumbled Stilton just before serving.

Alternatively, place the soup sprinkled with the crumbled Stilton under the broiler until the cheese has melted and starts to bubble. Serves 4-6.

Shelagh Aizlewood

See photograph page 32.

Korean Rice Cake Soup

1½ lbs. (750 g) beef, very thinly
    sliced
1 (1) bunch green onions,
    chopped
¼-½ tsp. (1-2 mL) garlic powder
¼ tsp. (1 mL) sesame oil
1-1½ tsp. (5-7 mL) regular oil
1¼-1½ cups (300-375 mL) Kikoman
    soy sauce
    salt and pepper to taste
2 qts. (2L) water
1 (1) pkg. Korean rice cakes*

Lorna McConnell

Mix beef, onions, garlic powder, both oils, 1 tbsp. (15 mL) soy sauce, salt and pepper in the bottom of a large soup pan. Cook on medium heat until the beef is browned. Add 2 quarts (2L) of water and leave to simmer for approximately 1½ hours. Add the rest of the soy sauce, according to taste.

Fifteen minutes before serving, add frozen rice cakes to the broth. Leave to simmer until the cakes are tender and chewy. Sprinkle with chopped green onions.

The longer this soup simmers the better it tastes. Always more delicious on the second day.

*Frozen rice cakes are available at Korean grocery stores, and at some Chinese stores.

Serves 4-6.

Lorna McConnell
Dancer
Alberta Ballet Company

See photograph page 32.

Lorna began her advanced dance training with the Royal Winnipeg Ballet and the Winnipeg Contemporary Dancers. She spent three years with the Minnesota Dance Theatre and then joined the Eddy Toussaint Dance Company in Montreal in 1980. She toured with that company to Eastern Canada, Martinique and Haiti. McConnell joined the Alberta Ballet Company in the 1982/3 season and has danced leading roles in Sacre Du Printemp and the full length Nutcracker as snow queen. Her performance of the step-mother in the full-length Cinderella showed brilliant comic timing and a great flair for the theatrical. She has also danced the role of fairy godmother in the same production of Cinderella.

Saucy Bouillabaisse

2 (2) cloves garlic, finely chopped
2 (2) onions, chopped
2 (2) sticks celery, chopped
2 (2) medium carrots, sliced
1 (1) small to medium green pepper, diced
3 tbsp. (50 mL) oil
1/4-1/2 lb. (125-250 g) fresh mushrooms OR 10 oz.
    (284 mL) can mushrooms with liquid
    dash of Tabasco
2 (2) bay leaves
    dash of ground cloves
1½ tsp. (7 mL) curry powder
½ tsp. (2 mL) basil
    salt, pepper to taste
2 cups (500 mL) chicken broth
28 oz. (796 mL) can tomatoes
2 lbs. (1 kg) fresh fillets (red snapper, cod,
    halibut, etc., more than 1 variety may be
    used)
12-15 (12-15) large shrimp

Sauté garlic, vegetables, except tomatoes and seasonings in oil. Add broth and tomatoes. Simmer 30 minutes. Add fish cut in large chunks and shrimp. Simmer another 10-15 minutes. Serve in bowls over rice.
Serves 4-6.

Claris Cowan
Administrative Staff
Alberta Ballet Company

Danish Soup

3 cups (750 mL) clear stock, bouillon cubes are
    fine
1 (1) medium onion, finely chopped
3 tbsp. (45 mL) butter
2 tsp. (10 mL) curry powder
4 tbsp. (60 mL) flour
4 oz. (115 g) white crab meat
4-6 oz. (115-170 g) peeled shrimp, fresh, tinned or
    frozen
1 tbsp. (15 mL) cream
2 tsp. (10 mL) dry sherry
    lemon twists
    chopped parsley, for garnish

Heat stock in 2-quart (2 L) saucepan. Then cook onions in melted butter until soft. Add curry powder, blending well. Then make a roux by blending in flour. Gradually add this mixture to the stock and stir until thick. Finally add the crab and shrimp.

Cook gently for approximately 15 minutes to blend the flavors thoroughly.

Before serving, add cream and sherry. Season to taste. Serve with a twist of lemon and a sprinkling of parsley.

Serves approximately 4.

Caroline de L. Davies

See photograph page 32.

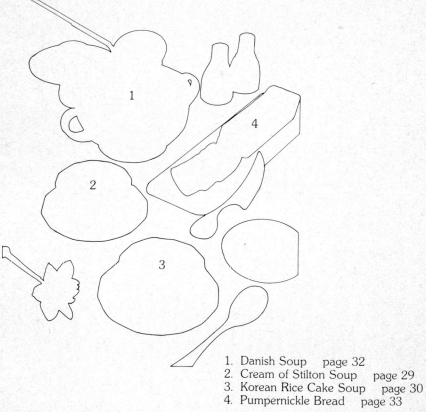

Pumpernickel Bread

This delicious bread is an inexpensive treat for people on the go.

    4 cups (1 L) 7 grain cereal
    1⅓ cups (325 mL) whole-wheat flour
    1 tbsp. (15 mL) baking soda
    1½ tbsp. (25 mL) salt
    ¾ cup (175 mL) of molasses
    4 cups (1 L) boiling water

In a large mixing bowl, combine the dry ingredients. Mix molasses and boiling water together. Then add to dry mixture, blending well. Cover and let stand overnight. Spoon batter into 2, 9" x 5" (23 cm x 13 cm) greased loaf pans. Cover with foil, sealing completely. Bake for 3 hours at 275°F (140°C).

Cool completely before removing from pan. May be stored in refrigerator for 1 week. This bread freezes well.

*No preservatives.

**7 grain cereal is available at most health shops.

Yields 2 loaves.

Stephen Lloyd
Former Apprentice with A.B.C.
Now at the Royal Winnipeg Ballet School

See photograph page 32.

Banana Bread

2¼ cups (550 mL) sugar
¾ cup (175 mL) of butter or
    margarine
3 (3) eggs
1½ cups (375 mL) mashed bananas
3 cups (750 mL) flour
1½ tbsp. (25 mL) baking powder
¾ tsp. (5 mL) salt
1½ (7 mL) tsp. soda
1 cup (250 mL) buttermilk
1½ tsp. (7 mL) vanilla

Cream sugar and butter or margarine. Add eggs and mashed bananas. Combine dry ingredients. Then add dry ingredients alternately with buttermilk. Stir in and add vanilla. Bake in 2 tube pans at 375°F (190°C) 1 hour. This bread is delicious and very moist.
Serves 14-20.

Liz McKale

Liz McKale

Executive Secretary to The Alberta Ballet Company and Fund Raising Assistant.

Salads
&
Vegetables

Orange and Chicory Salad

4 (4) oranges
12 oz. (340 g) white chicory (French endive)
  generous pinch of cayenne
3 tbsp. (45 mL) olive oil
1 tbsp. (15 mL) white wine vinegar
  salt, to taste
  freshly ground black pepper to taste
2 tbsp. (25 mL) finely chopped parsley
1 (1) head crisp round lettuce
  black olives, halved and stoned, for garnish

Peel oranges and cut into segments, removing all skin and pith. Work over a bowl to catch juices. Also squeeze remaining juices from orange scraps into bowl.

Separate each head of chicory into leaves. Wash and dry thoroughly.

Put cayenne into a small bowl. Whisk in oil slowly, then beat in vinegar and orange juice. Season to taste with salt and pepper and stir in parsley.

Wash lettuce carefully. Pat dry. Line 6 individual serving plates with lettuce leaves. Arrange chicory leaves in a shape on top of lettuce leaves. Place an orange segment in the hollow of each leaf. Spoon vinaigrette dressing over salad and decorate each plate with black olive halves.

Serve immediately.
Serves 6.

David MacGillivray
Dancer
Alberta Ballet Company

Tomato and Orange Salad with Sautéed Bananas

Brian Bender

Brian is a native of Salina, Kansas and his talents as a Martial Arts instructor led him to a career in classical dance.

He studied R.A.D. for three years with Valerie Roche at Creighton University of Omaha, Nebraska.

He joined the Alberta Ballet Company for the 1981/82 season and he has had leading roles in L'Histoire Du Soldat, Tzigane, the Nutcracker and the premiere of the Grand Pas De Dix from Raymonda. More recently in the Alberta Ballet Company's third residency at the Banff Centre, Bender danced principal roles in Sir Frederick Ashton's Facade and the Black Swan Pas De Deux staged by Laura Alonso of the National Ballet of Cuba. He is currently dancing with the Royal Winnipeg Ballet.

¾ lb. (340 g) tomatoes
2 (2) oranges, peeled
2 (2) small onions, finely chopped
6 tbsp. (90 mL) French vinaigrette dressing (see page 36)
1 (1) head of lettuce, washed
6 (6) firm bananas
Dijon mustard
freshly ground black pepper
6 (6) thin slices of lean bacon
3 tbsp. (45 mL) butter
6 (6) slices toast, buttered

Slice tomatoes, chop orange flesh into small pieces and add oranges and onions to the tomatoes. Pour French dressing over tomato mixture and set aside.

To serve, arrange lettuce leaves on serving plate, top with tomato, orange and onion mixture.

Peel bananas and brush with mustard. Sprinkle with pepper and wrap with bacon slices. Use skewers or toothpicks to secure bacon.

Melt butter in frying pan. Brown bananas gently on all sides in the hot fat, until the bacon is cooked.

Place bananas on toast slices and serve with Tomato and Orange Salad.
Serves 6.

Brian Bender
Dancer
Royal Winnipeg Ballet

Spinach Salad with Mustard Dressing

1 (1) large bunch of spinach, washed and stemmed
1 (1) large apple, unpeeled, cored and coarsely chopped
¼ cup (50 mL) peanuts
4 (4) eggs well beaten
½ cup (125 mL) sugar
¼ cup (50 mL) dry mustard
2 tsp. (10 mL) salt
2 cups (500 mL) whipping cream
⅔ cup (150 mL) white vinegar

Tear spinach leaves into large bowl, sprinkle with apple and peanuts. Then make the dressing.

Combine eggs, sugar, mustard, salt in medium bowl and mix well. Slowly stir in 1 cup (250 mL) whipping cream with vinegar. Transfer to heavy saucepan and cook slowly over medium heat until thickened. Remove from heat. Whisk in remaining cream.

Pour dressing over spinach salad. Toss thoroughly and serve.

**Dressing can be made in advance and refrigerated. Reheat before serving. Can be stored for up to 1 week. This amount of dressing is adequate for approximately 20 salad servings.
Serves 4-6.

Kim Derenne
Company Repetiteur, and
Assistant to the Artistic Director
Alberta Ballet Company

See photograph page 48.

Kim Derenne

Kim Derenne began his training in Wisconsin and continued at the North Carolina School of the Arts. Before that he had competed internationally as an Alpine Skier and small-boat sailor. He joined the Alberta Ballet Company for the 1977/78 season. The longest standing member of the Alberta Ballet Company, Derenne was appointed as Repetiteur and Assistant to the Artistic director in 1983. In that function, he accompanied his wife Mariane Beausejour, in May 1984, to Cuba where she danced with the National Ballet of Cuba and the Ballet Camaguey.

Renoir Salade

1 (1) head of romaine lettuce, torn into bite-size pieces
8 (8) raw spinach leaves, torn
12 (12) fresh mushrooms, sliced
1 cup (250 mL) shredded red cabbage
2 (2) tomatoes, sliced or quartered
4 (4) green onions, chopped
14 oz. (398 mL) can black olives, chopped or sliced
6 oz. (170 g) smoked salmon

French Mayonnaise Dressing

1 (1) egg yolk
1 tsp. (5 mL) lemon juice
¼ cup olive oil
¼ cup vegetable oil
⅛ tsp. (0.5 mL) garlic salt
1 tsp. (5 mL) salt
¼ tsp. (1 mL) pepper
½ tsp. (2 mL) sugar (optional)

Beat egg yolk with lemon juice and add the olive and vegetable oil gradually, beating all the time. Add the seasonings and beat again. The mayonnaise should have a thick creamy consistency.

Toss the vegetables together. Cut the smoked salmon into bite-size pieces, add to vegetables. Pour the mayonnaise over the salad, toss and serve.
Serves 4.

Anita Bostok
Dancer
Alberta Ballet Company

Anita Bostok

A native of Montreal, raised in California, Anita Bostok's extensive training in gymnastics led her towards a career in dance at the San Francisco Conservatory of Ballet under Merriam Lanova. Following her appearance at Ballet Celeste in Beau Danube, a work created by Leonide Massine, Bostok toured La Sylphide throughout France with Lanova in 1978. Upon her return to North America Bostok joined the Royal Winnipeg Ballet Professional Program. Prior to her joining the Alberta Ballet Company for the 1982/83 season, Bostok pursued further training at L'Ecole Superieure du Danse du Quebec.

Crunchy Kentucky Salad

  2 cups (500 mL) crushed pineapple
1½ cups (375 mL) of finely grated cucumber
2 x 3 oz. pkg. (2 x 85 g) lime gelatin dessert
      pineapple juice and water (enough to make 2
        cups (500 mL) of hot liquid)
  1 cup (250 mL) cold water
  1 tsp. (5 mL) lemon juice
    lettuce
    mayonnaise
    carrots, grated
    cherry tomatoes

Drain pineapple and cucumber. Make gelatin dessert according to package directions. Cool to consistency of egg whites. Fold in pineapple, cucumber and lemon juice. Pour into mold and refrigerate until firm. Unmold and serve on a bed of crisp lettuce, with mayonnaise. Garnish with grated carrot and cherry tomatoes. Serves 6-8.

Nancy Shainberg
Former Principal Dancer
Alberta Ballet Company

Tomatoes in Garlic Butter

16 (16) cherry tomatoes
3 tbsp. (45 mL) butter
2 tsp. (10 mL) garlic powder
2 tbsp. (25 mL) chopped parsley

Wash and clean cherry tomatoes. In a large skillet melt butter. Add garlic powder to melted butter. Over medium heat add the cherry tomatoes. Cook for 5 to 6 minutes gently moving the tomatoes around. Serve immediately.
Serves 4.

Lloyd Sutherland
President, Board of Directors
Alberta Ballet Company

See photograph page 48.

Hot Spiced Fruit

A colorful and delicious addition to roast pork, ham or chicken.

14 oz. (398 mL) can pear halves
14 oz. (398 mL) can apricot halves
19 oz. (540 mL) can pineapple tidbits
14 oz. (398 mL) can peach halves
10 oz. (284 mL) can mandarin oranges
   a few maraschino cherries
⅓ cup (75 mL) butter
¾ cup (175 mL) brown sugar
4 tsp. (20 mL) curry powder

Drain fruit and dry on paper towel. Arrange in a buttered casserole. Melt butter, add sugar and curry powder, spoon over fruit. Dot with butter. Bake at 300°F (150°C), uncovered, for 1 hour.
Serves 10-12.

The Hon. Mr. Peter Lougheed
Premier of Alberta

Spinach Loaf À La Bernoise

Delicious as an appetizer or accompaniment for roast chicken, veal or lamb.

2 (2) large bunches fresh spinach, well washed & stems removed
2 tbsp. (25 mL) unsalted butter
¼ cup (50 mL) finely minced green onions
2 (2) eggs
2 (2) egg yolks
1 cup (250 mL) half and half
½ cup (125 mL) bread crumbs
2-3 tbsp. (25-45 mL) freshly grated Parmesan cheese
⅛ tsp. (0.5 mL) nutmeg
½ tsp. (2 mL) salt
¼ tsp. (1 mL) pepper

2 tbsp. (25 mL) unsalted butter
½ lb. (250 g) mushroom caps, quartered
1 cup (250 mL) whipping cream
½ tsp. (2 mL) salt
¼ tsp. (1 mL) pepper
1 tbsp. (15 mL) butter and 1 tbsp. (15 mL) flour mixed into smooth paste
2 tbsp. (25 mL) finely minced chives for garnish

Cook spinach in rapidly boiling salted water 2-3 minutes. Drain thoroughly. When cool enough to handle, squeeze out all remaining moisture. Finely mince spinach and transfer to large mixing bowl.

Mariane Beausejour

Mariane Beausejour, a native of Quebec, studied as a full-scholarship student with L'Ecole Superieure of Les Grands Ballets Canadiens under the guidance of Ludmilla Chiriaeff, Fernand Nault and Brian Macdonald. Beausejour was representative of Canada at the First International Ballet Seminar in Varna, Bulgaria. She joined the Alberta Ballet Company in 1978.

In 1984, Beausejour travelled to Cuba where she guested with Alicia Alonso's world renowned National Ballet of Cuba. She then went on to the Camaguey Ballet of Cuba and danced Lise in the full-length La Fille Mal Gardee as well as Odette in Swan Lake.

Spinach Loaf À La Bernoise (cont'd.)

Preheat oven to 350°F (180°C). Generously butter 9" x 5" (23 cm x 13 cm) loaf pan and line with buttered waxed paper. Melt butter in small heavy skillet over medium heat. Add green onions and sauté 2-3 minutes until softened but not brown. Add to spinach.

Combine eggs, egg yolks and half and half in small mixing bowl and blend thoroughly with whisk. Add to spinach mixture together with breadcrumbs, Parmesan, nutmeg, salt and pepper. Spoon into prepared loaf pan and place in large baking dish. Add boiling water to outer dish to depth of 1" (2.5 cm). Cover loaf pan loosely with foil and bake 50 minutes or until knife comes out clean. Remove from oven and set aside.

Melt remaining 2 tbsp. (25 mL) butter in large skillet over medium heat, add mushrooms, sauté 2-3 minutes until nicely browned. Add cream, salt and pepper and bring to boil.

Gradually whisk in bits of butter-flour mixture, beating constantly until sauce lightly coats spoon. Remove from heat and stir in chives. Run knife around edges of spinach loaf and unmold onto rectangular serving plate.

Discard waxed paper. Cut loaf into slices. Spoon mushroom sauce over and garnish with chives.
Serves 4-6.

Mariane Beausejour
Principal Dancer
Alberta Ballet Company

See photograph page 64.

43

Gourmet Wild Rice and Cheese Casserole

1   cup (250 mL) wild rice
¼   tsp. (1 mL) salt
3   cups (750 mL) boiling water
½   lb. (500 g) mushrooms, sliced [about 3 cups
      (750 mL)]
½   cup (125 mL) chopped onion
½   cup (125 mL) butter
1   cup (250 mL) grated old Cheddar cheese
19 oz. (540 mL) can tomatoes
1   tsp. (5 mL) salt

Cook rice, covered, in boiling salted water until nearly tender, about 30 minutes. Drain rice if necessary. Sauté mushrooms and onion in butter for about 5 minutes. Toss rice with all ingredients. Place in buttered 2-quart (2 L) casserole. Cover and bake 1 hour at 350°F (180°C).

This may be prepared the day before and baked just before serving. Serve as a vegetable with pork, poultry or game.
Serves 6-8.

The Hon. Mr. Peter Lougheed
Premier of Alberta

Entrées

Shrimp and Snow Peas

Please include in Ballet *Grass Widowers* section. Certain husbands have supported the ABC in some obscure but significant ways, e.g., whipping up tasty little noshes for wives about to rush off to the Jubilee auditorium to feed dancers, or concocting meals to eat in the mad dash before an 8:00 p.m. performance.

1 (1) medium-size pkg. large, frozen, shelled, deveined shrimp/prawns
1 (1) medium onion, sliced obliquely
2 (2) green onions, sliced obliquely
1 (1) tiny clove fresh garlic, minced
1 (1) medium green pepper seeded and sliced obliquely
⅛ tsp. (0.5 mL) ginger powder, or to taste
⅛ tsp. (0.5 mL) curry powder, or to taste
⅛ tsp. (0.5 mL) salt, or to taste
ground black pepper — about 6 grinds
15-20 (15-20) snow pea pods, fresh preferred

Thaw shrimp and wash, pat dry. In a skillet, pan or wok, over medium-high heat, sauté the 2 kinds of onion and garlic until translucent. Add green pepper strips and stir-fry. Add shrimp, ginger, curry powder, salt, pepper, stir-fry 2 minutes then add snow peas. Stir-fry 1 minute. Serve immediately with rice or Chinese noodles.
Serves 2 (may be doubled for 4 or 6).

Michael Hamer

Shrimp Stroganoff

Alexandra Danilova

An internationally known Russian dancer, Alexandra Davilova now teaches at the American Ballet Theatre with Mikhail Barishnykov.

Born in St. Petersburg, she was trained at the School of Imperial/ State Ballet in St. Petersburg/Petrograd. She toured with George Balanchine to Western Europe. In Paris they joined the Diaghilev Ballet Russe. She became a charter member of the Ballet Russe De Monte Carlo in 1933.

Her role in the film "Turning Point" won her a new audience of fans. As a beloved teacher at the School of American Ballet Theatre, she has choreographed a production of "Coppelia", always her great success with Balanchine, for the New York City Ballet.

1	lb. (500 g) shrimp, peeled and cleaned.
6	tbsp. (90 mL) butter or margarine
1	(1) medium onion, chopped
10	oz. (284 mL) can sliced mushrooms, drained
2	tbsp. (25 mL) tomato paste
6	tbsp. (90 mL) sour cream
1	(1) bay leaf
2-3	(2-3) peppercorns
½	tsp. (2 mL) salt, or to taste

Cook the shrimp in boiling water, just until pink. Melt the butter or margarine in a pan and cook the onion until transparent, then add the drained mushrooms. Mix in the tomato paste and cook for 15 minutes on a low heat. Add sour cream and shrimp, mix well. Add the bay leaf, peppercorns and salt to taste. Cook over a low heat for approximately 20 minutes. Serve with rice, Tomatoes in Garlic Butter, see page 41, and broccoli.
Serves 4.

Madame Alexandra Danilova
Teacher / Choreographer
American Ballet Theatre

Crab Supreme

3 x 6½ oz. (3 - 195 g) cans crab
½ cup (125 mL) chopped celery
½ cup (125 mL) chopped onions
2 x 2 oz. (2 x 60 g) jars pimiento (optional)
½ cup (125 mL) mayonnaise
salt, pepper to taste
½ tsp. (2 mL) dry mustard
12 (12) slices white bread (no crusts)
butter (to spread on bread)
1½ lbs. (750 g) grated Swiss cheese
5 (5) eggs
3 (750 mL) milk

Toss crab with celery, onions, pimiento. Add mayonnaise, salt, pepper and mustard. Spread bread generously with butter on both sides. In 9" x 13" (23 cm x 33 cm) baking pan, layer bread slices, then crab mixture, then grated cheese. Repeat 2 layers of each. Beat eggs and milk and pour over casserole. Cover and let stand overnight or at least 3 hours in refrigerator. Bake uncovered 1 hour at 325°F (160°C). Serving suggestions for a luncheon or light supper include avocado salad, white wine and a fresh fruit dessert.
Serves 9-10.

Sandra Currie
Soloist
Alberta Ballet Company

See photograph on front cover.

Sandra Currie

Sanda Currie trained at the Anna Wyman studio in Vancouver with Diane Milles, and Chiat Goh, former ballet master with Anna Wyman, and principal dancer with the Peking Ballet of China. In 1978, Ms. Currie joined the newly formed Goh Ballet which toured as far afield as Singapore. She joined the Alberta Ballet Company in Banff for the 1982/83 season, and since then has received critical acclaim for roles in Pineapple Poll, Nut-cracker, Sundances and many others.

1. Honey Curry Chicken   page 53
2. Tomatoes in Garlic Butter   page 41
3. Spinach Salad with Mustard Dressing   page 38

Spaghetti With Crab

Arnold Spohr

Arnold Spohr, was born in Saskatchewan.

Joining the Royal Winnipeg Ballet in 1945 he rose to the rank of premier danseur, creating roles in over twenty ballets. His dancing career culminated as a partner to Dame Alicia Markova.

Spohr accepted the position as Artistic Director in 1958, when the company was attempting to survive its most severe crisis. He commissioned new ballets; established associations with ballet companies abroad, helped launch the company's own school in Winnipeg and is largely responsible for the R.W.B.'s outstanding reputation.

1983 marked Arnold Spohr's 25th season as Artistic Director.

1 lb. (500 g) fresh spaghetti
1 tbsp. (15 mL) olive oil
2 tbsp. (25 mL) butter
8 oz. (250 g) crab, chopped in chunks
1 tbsp. (15 mL) white wine
2 tbsp. (25 mL) chicken stock
1 tbsp. (15 mL) lemon juice
1 cup (250 mL) whipping cream
½ cup (125 mL) Parmesan cheese
3 tbsp. (45 mL) chopped fresh parsley

Cook fresh spaghetti al dente, 3-5 minutes in lots of boiling water. I recommend adding a 1 tbsp. (15 mL) of olive oil to the water to help keep the spaghetti separate.

Melt butter in large skillet. Add crab and cook for 2-3 minutes, stirring occasionally. Add white wine, chicken stock and lemon juice. Simmer for 1-2 minutes. Add whipping cream, stirring with wire whisk to ensure everything is well blended. Simmer for 2-3 minutes to reduce slightly.

Add the spaghetti to the sauce, ⅓ at a time, mixing to coat between each addition. With each addition, include a portion of the Parmesan, leaving a couple of spoonfuls to sprinkle on top. When spaghetti is piping hot, transfer to bowl or platter and sprinkle the parsley and Parmesan on top. Serve with garlic bread and your favorite salad.

Sea legs may be substituted for crab, however, chop them finely in the food processor for a better look.

Note: Pasta should always be added to sauce, *not* sauce to pasta.
Serves 4-6.

Arnold Spohr
Artistic Director
Royal Winnipeg Ballet

Coquilles St. Jacques

2 lbs. (1 kg) scallops
2 cups (500 mL) white wine
1 (1) bay leaf
¼ tsp. (1 mL) thyme
1 (1) celery leaf
3 (3) sprigs parsley
1 tsp. (5 mL) salt
6 tbsp. (75 mL) butter
½ cup (125 mL) chopped mushrooms
6 (6) green onions, chopped
1 tbsp. (15 mL) finely chopped parsley
1 tsp. (5 mL) bottled lemon juice
¼ cup (50 mL) water
3 (3) egg yolks
½ cup (125 mL) cream
4 tbsp. (50 mL) flour
½ cup (125 mL) fine dry bread crumbs
4 tbsp. (50 mL) grated Parmesan cheese OR
4 tbsp. (50 mL) grated Swiss cheese

If frozen, thaw scallops just enough to separate. Simmer next 6 ingredients for 5 minutes. Add scallops and simmer for 8 minutes. Drain, reserving broth, and chop scallops coarsely. (Small scallops may be left whole.) Melt 2 tbsp. (25 mL) of the butter in a saucepan; add mushrooms, onions, parsley, lemon juice and water. Mix well, cover and simmer 10 minutes over medium heat. Strain, reserving vegetables and add liquid to wine broth. Beat egg yolks with cream. Melt remaining 4 tbsp. (50 mL) butter in saucepan, add flour and mix well. Add combined liquids and cook over a medium heat, stirring constantly for 3-4 minutes, or until creamy smooth. Remove from the heat, stir in egg yolk mixture with a whisk or wooden spoon. Taste for seasoning, stir in scallops, green onions and mushrooms. Heap this thick mixture into scallop shells or individual dishes and sprinkle with bread crumbs and cheese, previously mixed together. Bake in 450°F (230°C) oven for 5-8 minutes or until brown on top.
Serves 6-8.

Colleen Smith
Former Dancer with A.B.C.
Now at the Royal Winnipeg Ballet School

Sole St. André Au Whisky

¼ lb. (115 g) prawns in shells
½ lb. (250 g) butter
4 (4) small sole
2 tbsp. (25 mL) flour
4 tbsp. (60 mL) whisky (Scotch)
¾ cup (175 mL) whipping cream
½ tsp. (2 mL) salt
¼ tsp. (1 mL) pepper
few grains of cayenne
lemon wedges for garnish

Shell prawns and reserve. Put prawn shells through finest blade of mincer and cream thoroughly with half of the butter. Reserve the prawn butter.

Trim sole. Sprinkle with flour. Simmer in remaining butter in a shallow pan until cooked, about 5-8 minutes. Do not let them color. When sole is ready, arrange on heated serving dish. Pour off cooking butter and pour whisky into pan, scraping all crunchy bits from the bottom and sides of pan. Add cream and prawn butter and cook, stirring continuously until sauce is reduced. Season with salt, pepper and cayenne and strain over sole. Warm shelled prawns then sprinkle over sole, and garnish with lemon wedges.

Serves 4.

Caroline de L. Davies

Salmon — Hot or Cold

This is my mother's recipe and is an extremely simple but delicious method for preparing salmon.

1 (1) salmon or piece of salmon
2 tbsp. (25 mL) malt vinegar
2 tbsp. (25 mL) salt

In a covered pan, large enough to hold the fish, put enough water to cover the fish. Add the malt vinegar and salt. Bring to the boil. Put in the salmon, cover with a lid and cook for exactly 3 minutes.

Remove from the burner and let it stay in the covered pan for exactly 1 hour.

Serve at once if you wish it to be hot, or take it out of the water and chill if you prefer it cold.

Betty Farrally
Founder
Royal Winnipeg Ballet

Apprenticeship Special!

8 oz. (225 g) box Kraft Dinner
6.5 oz. (184 g) can flaked light tuna

Prepare the Kraft Dinner according to the instructions on the box. Once the cheese and milk have mixed with the cooked macaroni, drain the can of tuna and mix in thoroughly. Serve warm.

If unexpected guests arrive, add 1 cup (250 mL) of frozen peas to increase the volume!

Serves 2-3.

Clark Blakley
Royal Winnipeg Ballet School

Honey Curry Chicken

Brydon Paige

A native of Vancouver, British Columbia, Brydon Paige became one of the founding members of Ballets Chiriaeff in Montreal in 1952. He was principal character dancer when the company evolved into Les Grands Ballets Canadiens. In 1976, Paige accepted the position of Artistic Director of the Alberta Ballet Company and deliberately set out to build a company that concentrated on both contemporary and classical works. He has also worked with the National Ballet of Portugal, the National Arts Centre in Ottawa, and the Banff School of Fine Arts. He has choreographed and appeared in numerous operas and television productions in Montreal, Ottawa, Quebec, Toronto, Edmonton, and Calgary.

This recipe is not originally mine but I pinched it from Margo Oliver. It became the hit of Philadelphia's Pennsylvania Ballet. It is totally foolproof (unless you forget and go away for a few days) and guaranteed to win friends and influence people.

⅓ cup (75 mL) butter
½ cup (125 mL) honey
¼ cup (50 mL) mustard (ordinary hot-dog kind)
4 tsp. (20 mL) curry powder
1 (1) frying chicken cut up into pieces, skin removed

In 275°F (140°C) oven, melt the butter in a large flat pan — remove pan from oven add all other ingredients and stir until smooth. Add chicken pieces and slosh around until well coated with sauce. Place skin-side down in pan. Heat oven to 375°F (190°C), bake chicken pieces uncovered for ¾ hour. Turn pieces over and cook additional 15 minutes, or until nicely done. Remove and serve.

Serve with a green salad, rice and Tomatoes in Garlic Butter, see page 41. With its subtle taste of curry, this chicken is just as tasty cold. It is perfect for a picnic lunch.
Serves 4.

Brydon Paige
Artistic Director
Alberta Ballet Company

See photograph page 48.

Chicken Paprika

1½ tbsp. (22 mL) butter
1½ tbsp. (22 mL) cooking oil
  1 cup (250 mL) chopped onions
  2 tsp. - 2 tbsp. (10-25 mL) paprika, according to
      taste
  ½ tsp. (2 mL) salt
  2 cups (500 mL) well-seasoned stock
2½ lb. (1 kg) chicken, cut in pieces
  1 tsp. (5 mL) flour
  1 cup (250 mL) sour cream

In a heavy saucepan melt the butter and oil. Add the chopped onions and simmer until golden color. Then add the paprika to taste.

Add the salt and seasoned stock and bring to a boil, then add the chicken pieces and simmer, covered, until tender. (About 1 hour).

Stir flour into sour cream. Stir it slowly into the pot. Cook for a further 5 minutes to heat thoroughly but do not boil. Serve at once, with noodles or rice.
Serves 3-4.

Clark Blakley
Royal Winnipeg Ballet School

Velvet Chicken

David La Hay

David La Hay was born in Barrie, Ontario. He holds a B.A. from Trent University in Peterborough and an Honours B.F.A. in dance from York University. While still a student, he danced with the Toronto Regional Ballet of Diana Jablokova Vorps. David joined Les Grands Ballets Canadiens' Compagnons de la Danse in 1973, and the Company in 1974.

In 1973, he received a Canada Council grant to study in New York with Finis Jhung. In 1975, he went to London to study with Anna Northcotte. In 1977, he danced with the Atlanta Ballet. A year later, he became a principal dancer with Les Grands Ballets Canadiens and was invited to dance at the Cuban International Dance Festival that same year.

Can be prepared in advance and simmered gently while guests arrive.

2 **tbsp. (25 mL) oil**
2 **tbsp. (25 mL) butter**
3-4 **lbs. (1.5-2 kg) chicken pieces**
2 **(2) medium tomatoes, quartered**
1½ **tsp. (7 mL) salt**
1 **(1) medium-sized onion, quartered**
1 **(1) clove garlic**
¼ **tsp. (1 mL) pepper**
1 **(1) carrot, cut up**
1 **(1) stalk of celery, cut up**
6 **(6) sprigs fresh parsley**
¼ **cup (50 mL) white wine**
½ **tsp. (2 mL) rosemary**
¼ **tsp. (1 mL) tarragon**
1 **cup (250 mL) cup sliced mushrooms**

Heat oil and butter in large frying pan. Sauté chicken over medium heat until browned on all sides. Drain off fat.

Meanwhile, put tomatoes, salt, onion, garlic, pepper, carrot and celery in blender.

Blend for a few seconds, then add parsley, wine, rosemary and tarragon.

Blend on high speed for 30 seconds. Pour over chicken in frying pan, cover and simmer for 45 minutes, add mushrooms ½ hour before serving. Potato nests filled with peas or rice and stuffed green peppers would complement this dish. Serves 4.

David La Hay
Principal Dancer
Les Grands Ballets Canadiens

Chicken & Black Cherries

This is a quick and easy way of making a special meal for unexpected guests. It is also inexpensive.

2½-3 lb. (1-1.5 kg) roasting chicken
14 oz. (398 mL) tin black cherries, pitted
4-5 tbsp. (60-75 mL) sherry
2 tbsp. (25 mL) flour

Put chicken in a roasting pan with a little fat and ½ the sherry, cover with foil and roast at 350°F (180°C) for approximately 1-1½ hours, basting frequently. When cooked, remove chicken from pan and place on serving dish. Keep warm.

Skim fat from pan, make a roux by blending the remaining juices and the flour. Add the cherry juice and remaining sherry. Then add the stoned cherries and simmer until warmed through. Pour sauce over the chicken and serve. Wild or long-grain rice and broccoli are perfect accompaniments.
Serves 4-6.

Allan Barry
Soloist
Alberta Ballet Company

Allan Barry

A native of Christchurch, New Zealand, Allan Barry began his ballet training at the age of seven. Upon his graduation, in 1980, from the New Zealand School of Dance, he joined the New Zealand Ballet and was later promoted to soloist. Prior to his joining the Alberta Ballet Company for the 1983/84 season, Barry was a member of the Banff Centre Dance Festival under the direction of Brian Macdonald. His performance as the Blue Boy in Les Patineurs, produced by Alexander Grant, received national acclaim. In 1983/84, he danced the Prince in Brydon Paige's highly successful Nutcracker and also appeared in Cinderella, as well as the premiere of Lambros Lambrou's Tzigane.

Mock Veal

This recipe tastes just like veal — perfect for supper parties when surviving on a low budget.

4 (4) bunches fresh spinach/or 3 x 10 oz. (3 x 284 g) boxes frozen chopped spinach
few drops of lemon juice
½ lb. (250 g) large mushrooms
2 tbsp. (25 mL) butter
2 (2) whole boneless chicken breasts (approx. 2 lbs.) (1 kg)
¼ cup (50 mL) melted butter
¼ cup (50 mL) flour
1 tsp. (5 mL) salt
¼ tsp. (1 mL) pepper
¼ tsp. (1 mL) powdered chicken stock
1 cup (250 mL) whipping cream
½ cup (125 mL) freshly grated Parmesan cheese

Wash and pick over fresh spinach carefully. Wilt spinach in large kettle by heating (without adding water) over a low heat. Cool, squeeze liquid from spinach and chop coarsely with knife or food processor. If using frozen spinach, cook according to directions. Cool, squeeze dry. Arrange evenly in bottom of buttered au gratin dish, or shallow baking dish. Sprinkle with few drops of lemon juice.

Wash mushrooms and pat dry, chop coarsely. Sauté mushrooms in 2 tbsp. (25 mL) butter over a low heat until limp. Set aside. Separate chicken breasts. Slice each single piece horizontally twice — you will now have 8 pieces. Remove from heat and dip chicken pieces in melted butter, then in flour to coat. Arrange chicken on top of spinach in a single layer. Top with the mushrooms, sprinkle with salt and pepper. Sprinkle the chicken stock and pour the cream over everything. Sprinkle evenly with grated Parmesan cheese. Bake in a preheated 400°F (200°C) for 20 minutes. Serve at once.

Great with cooked noodles and buttered carrots flavored with nutmeg and a dash of ginger.
Serves 6.

Caroline de L. Davies

Wild Duck in Orange and Lemon Gravy

1 (1) large duck
1 (1) strip orange peel
1 (1) strip lemon peel
2 oz. (60 g) butter
6 tbsp. (75 mL) oil
¼ cup (50 mL) flour
2 cups (500 mL) beef broth
1 tbsp. (15 mL) ground coriander
½ tsp. (2 mL) freshly ground
      peppercorns
1 tsp. (5 mL) salt
   juice of 2 (2) oranges
   juice of ½ (½) lemon

Prepare the duck for roasting.

Place the strips of orange and lemon peel in the cavity of the body. Brown the bird for about 10 minutes in melted butter and oil, using a large metal baking dish and a moderately high heat. Remove the bird temporarily. Reduce the heat.

Turn oven on at 350°F (180°C).

Blend ¼ cup (50 mL) flour with residue in the bottom of the baking dish by stirring and scraping. Add the beef broth slowly. Then add the coriander, pepper, and salt.

Replace the bird in the oven, bake uncovered for 1½ hours or until tender. Add orange and lemon juice. Cook uncovered for 10 minutes. Remove the bird. Skim off excess fat. Strain gravy if desired. Boil to reduce to proper consistency. Serve duck topped with gravy. With this Spinach Loaf à La Bernoise page 42, is delicious.
Serves 4-6.

Scott Harris
Principal Dancer
Alberta Ballet Company

See photograph page 64.

Scott Harris

A native of Edmonton, Scott Harris began his early training at the Muriel Taylor School of Dance. He studied at the Royal Winnipeg Ballet Professional program and the National Ballet School in Toronto.

Harris joined the Alberta Ballet Company for the 1981/82 season, after his return from the National Arts Centre in Ottawa where he appeared as a soloist in the highly acclaimed Idomeneo, choreographed by Brydon Paige.

Harris performed at the International Ballet Festival in Havana, Cuba in the fall of 1984 with Mariane Beausejour, and received well deserved acclaim.

Harris marks his first season as principal dancer with the Alberta Ballet Company in 1984/85.

Baked Spareribs

These spareribs taste even better the following day.

4 lbs. (2 kg) side or back spareribs
2 tbsp. (25 mL) lemon juice
2 (2) medium onion, finely chopped
1 tsp. (5 mL) salt
½ tsp. (2 mL) pepper
1 tsp. (5 mL) celery salt
2 tsp. (10 mL) chili powder
¼ cup (50 mL) brown sugar
¼ cup (50 mL) vinegar
2 tbsp. (25 mL) soy sauce
2 tbsp. (25 mL) Worcestershire sauce
1 cup (250 mL) tomato ketchup
2 cups (500 mL) water
3-4 drops (3-4) Tabasco sauce

Cut ribs into 2-rib pieces. Arrange in a shallow baking pan. Sprinkle with lemon juice, onion, salt and pepper. Bake for 30 minutes at 425°F (220°C). To prepare sauce, combine all remaining ingredients in saucepan. Simmer 30 minutes, then pour over ribs. Reduce oven heat to 350°F (180°C). Bake ribs for 1 hour. Delicious with baked or French-fried potatoes, a tossed salad and corn on the cob.
Serves 4-6.

Lloyd Sutherland
President, Board of Directors
Alberta Ballet Company

Spicy Roast Pork

3 lbs. (1.5 kg) pork roast
½ cup (125 mL) orange juice
¼ cup (50 mL) soy sauce
1 tsp. (5 mL) 5 spice powder
1 tsp. (5 mL) allspice
1 tsp. (5 mL) ground ginger
½ tsp. (2 mL) black pepper
½ tsp. (2 mL) paprika
3 tsp. (15 mL) salt
1 (1) medium onion, finely chopped
½ tsp. (2 mL) finely chopped garlic
2 tsp. (10 mL) brown sugar
2 tsp. (10 mL) sweet chili sauce (Yeo's Oriental)

Wipe roast and, using a sharp knife, make about 6 small slits, approximately 2'' (5 cm) deep in each side of the pork. Combine the orange juice and soy sauce and set aside.

Combine all other ingredients in a small bowl and using a teaspoon, stuff the slits in the roast. Pour on the orange/soy sauce mixture and marinate overnight in a tightly closed container. Bake in a covered pan for approximately 2 hours at 350°F (180°C).

Baste occasionally and remove lid for the last ½ hour of cooking.

Delicious with Gourmet Wild Rice and Cheese Casserole, page 44.

Serves 6-8.

Charmaine Bucknor

60

Lamb Chops in Piquant Sauce

Ruth Carse

Ruth Carse has been called "Alberta's First Lady of Dance." She has danced in New York City, London and Toronto. After almost forty years as a dancer and teacher, she has earned the love and respect of Canada's dance community. Determined to change a lifeless cultural scene in Edmonton, Miss Carse formed a small amateur dance troupe called Dance Interlude. In 1960, Dance Interlude became the Edmonton Ballet, which evolved into the Alberta Ballet Company in 1966, with a reputation of providing the highest quality dance entertainment. Miss Carse is a lifetime member of the Board of Directors of the Alberta Ballet Company and full-time Director of the Alberta Ballet School.

juice of 1 (1) lemon
2 tbsp. (25 mL) red currant jelly
1 tbsp. (15 mL) Worcestershire sauce
⅛ tsp. (0.5 mL) nutmeg
5 (5) lamb chops
1 tbsp. (15 mL) flour
1 tbsp. (15 mL) cold water

In a bowl, mix the lemon juice, red currant jelly, Worcestershire sauce and nutmeg.

Brown chops on both sides — about 5-10 minutes. Put them in a greased 1½-2-quart casserole dish. Cover with sauce and bake 1¼ hours at 350°F (180°C).

Just before serving, mix flour with cold water. Remove chops from dish and thicken the sauce with the flour. Return chops to sauce and serve.

**For more than 5 chops, double the other ingredients.

Serves 2.

Ruth Carse
Founder
Alberta Ballet Company

Roast Leg of Lamb With Orzo

Lambros Lambrou

6½ - 7 lb. (3-3.5 kg) leg of lamb, trim of excess fat but leave on parchment-like covering
1 (1) large garlic clove, peeled and cut lengthwise into 8 thin slivers
1 tsp. (5 mL) oregano, crumbled
2 tsp. (10 mL) salt
   freshly ground black pepper
6 tbsp. (75 mL) fresh lemon juice
2 (2) medium-sized onions, peeled and thinly sliced
1 cup (250 mL) boiling water
2 cups (1 lb.) (500 mL or 450g) ORZO (rice-shaped pasta)
½ cup (125 mL) tomato purée
   freshly grated KEFALOTIRI or imported Parmesan cheese

Preheat the oven to 450°F (230°C). With the tip of a small sharp knife, make 8, ¼" deep incisions on the fat side of the lamb and insert the slivers of garlic. Combine the oregano, 1 tsp. (5 mL) salt and a few grindings of pepper and press the mixture firmly all over the surface of the lamb.

Place the leg, fat side up, on a rack in a shallow roasting pan and roast it uncovered in the middle of the oven for 20 minutes. Reduce the heat to 350°F (180°C), baste the leg with 1 tablespoon (15 mL) of lemon juice and scatter the onions in the bottom of the pan. Roast for 15 minutes and then baste with another tablespoon (15 mL) of lemon juice and pour the cup (250 mL) of boiling

Lambrou was born in Cyprus and studied dance there with his sister Nadia Nicolaides. In 1973 in London, England he trained at the Arts Education School, followed by a scholarship at the Royal Ballet School. He accepted a contract with the Alberta Ballet Company in 1975.

Lambrou's works have been included in the repertoires of the Royal Winnipeg Ballet, North Carolina Dance Theatre, the Richmond Ballet and the National Ballet of Cuba.

Lambrou has worked in Australia, choreographing and re-staging ballets for the West Australian Ballet. He has been asked to return there in 1985.

Lambrou is also the director of the professional program of the Alberta Ballet School.

Roast Leg of Lamb With Orzo
(cont'd.)

water over the onion. Basting the meat periodically with the lemon juice, continue roasting for another 40 to 60 minutes, or until the lamb is done to your taste.

(The Greeks prefer well-done lamb)

Meanwhile bring 2 quarts (2 L) of water and the remaining teaspoon (5 mL) of salt to a boil over a high heat. Pour in the Orzo in a slow stream so that the water doesn't stop boiling, and cook briskly for about 10 minutes until the Orzo is tender but still slightly resistant to the bite. Drain in a colander.

When the lamb is done, place it on a large heated platter and let it rest at room temperature for 10-15 minutes before carving.

Meanwhile, pour off all but a thin film of fat from the roasting pan. Stir the tomato purée into the onions, scraping in any brown particles clinging to the bottom and sides of the pan. Stir in the Orzo, return the pan to the middle shelf of the oven and bake uncovered for 10-15 minutes until the Orzo is heated through. Taste for seasoning.

To serve, mound the Orzo around the leg of lamb and pass the grated cheese separately to be sprinkled over the pasta.
Serves 8.

Lambros Lambrou
Resident Choreographer
Alberta Ballet Company

Chateaubriand with Espagnole Sauce

3 lbs. (1.5 kg) centre-cut beef fillet
salt to taste
olive oil
red pepper, cut in strips
parsley

Trim fat and skin from fillet and flatten with a broad blade cleaver. Sprinkle with salt and brush with oil, broil for 20 minutes. Remove to platter, garnish with red pepper and parsley. Serve with Espagnole Sauce.

Espagnole Sauce

1 (1) onion, sliced
2 (2) carrots sliced
1 (1) shallot, finely chopped
1 (1)whole clove
8 (8) peppercorns
bit of bay leaf
2 tbsp. (25 mL) butter
3 tbsp. (45 mL) flour
1 cup (250 mL) brown stock (bouillon, or any
type of meat concentrate)
salt and pepper to taste

Cook vegetables and seasonings with butter until well browned. Stir in flour and brown. Add stock, bring to boiling point. Season with salt and pepper. Let simmer until ready to pour over steak, approximately 10-15 minutes. This sauce may also be used to flavor less expensive cuts of meat.
Serves 6-8.

Steven Findlay
Former Apprentice
Alberta Ballet Company

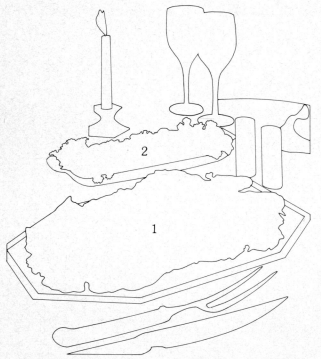

Carbonnade of Beef

2 lb. (1 kg) good quality stewing steak
4 tbsp. (60 mL) seasoned flour (plain flour with
    salt & pepper added)
4 tbsp. (60 mL) butter or margarine
3 tbsp. (45 mL) oil
2 (2) medium-sized onions
1 (1) clove garlic (optional)
4 oz. (115 g) mushrooms
2¼ oz. (65 g) can tomato pureé
1½ cups (375 mL) Guinness
1½ cups (375 mL) water
1 tsp. (5mL) vinegar
2-3 (2-3) bay leaves

Preheat oven to 300°F (150°C), place oven rack in centre.

Trim the meat and cut into neat chunky cubes

Place in a sturdy paper or polythene bag with seasoned flour.

Shake well, until pieces of meat are coated in flour. Reserve any excess.

Melt the butter or margarine and oil in saucepan.

Fry meat till brown on all sides, stirring frequently.

Prepare onions and slice thinly.

Peel and crush clove of garlic (if used).

Prepare and slice mushrooms.

Add onion, garlic and mushrooms to frying pan, cook 2-3 minutes.

Stir in any remaining seasoned flour and the tomato pureé.

Stir in Guinness, water, vinegar, bay leaves and seasoning if liked.

Bring to the boil and pour into an oven-proof 4-quart (4 L) casserole.

Cover and cook in the oven on the centre shelf for between 2 and 3 hours, or until meat is tender. Can be served over buttered noodles or baked potato.

**I find it is better to let the meat sit in the Guinness, water, and vinegar for at least 4 hours before cooking it in the oven. That way it is marinated and tastes so much nicer.

Serves 4-6.

Caroline de L. Davies

Beef Stroganoff

1½ lbs. (750 g) beef
6 tbsp. (75 mL) butter
1 (1) medium-sized onion, chopped
½ lb. (250 g) mushrooms or 10 oz. can (284 mL)
3-5 (3-5) peppercorns
1 (1) bay leaf
10 oz. can (284 mL) mushroom soup
1 cup (250 mL) sour cream
1 tbsp. (15 mL) Worcestershire sacuce
salt to taste

Cut the beef in small pieces, approximately 2" (5cm) long and 1" (2.5 cm) thick. Melt the butter in a frying pan, and fry onions until they are transparent. Fry mushrooms in the same pan, add meat and cook on all sides. Pour into a deep 2-quart (2L) casserole dish. Add peppercorns, bay leaf and mushroom soup. Mix well and then add sour cream and Worcestershire sauce. Add salt to taste. Cook over a moderate heat until the meat is tender. Garnish with chopped parsley.

Serve with rice and steamed broccoli, cauliflower and carrots. This dish can be made a day ahead, the flavor improves overnight. Serves 6-8.

Madame Alexandra Danilova
Teacher/Choreographer
American Ballet Theatre

See photograph on back cover.

Casserole for Underpaid Artists

Celia Franca

Franca received her early training at the Guildhall School of Music, then studied with Noreen Bush, Judith Espinosa, Marie Rambert, Anthony Tudor and Vera Volkova, then entered the Sadler's Wells Ballet.

She performed with the Ballet Rambert from 1936 to 1939, and with the Sadler's Wells Ballet from 1940-1945.

In 1951 she became Artistic Director of the National Ballet of Canada. She remained until 1974, choreographing and performing in mime and character roles. Even after retiring she continued to coach dancers and teach.

Celia Franca has received the Order of Canada for her services to the world of dance.

1	lb. (500 g) ground beef
1	(1) medium onion, chopped
	a little butter or margarine
	pepper, to taste
	Lawry's Seasoned Salt, to taste
2	cups (500 mL) frozen peas, thawed
1	cup (250 mL) chopped celery
19	oz. (540 mL) can cream of mushroom soup
	potato chips for topping

Brown beef and chopped onion in butter in pan. Pour off any extra fat. Season to taste with pepper and Lawry's Seasoned Salt.

Place beef/onion mixture in bottom of casserole. Layer peas on top of beef. Layer celery on top of peas. Pour mushroom soup, undiluted, over beef, celery and pea layers. Top with crumbled potato chips.

Bake in 350°F (180°C) oven for 1 hour. Serve with rice or noodles and a colorful vegetable such as carrots, corn or stuffed tomatoes. Worcestershire sauce may be enjoyed on individual servings.

Serves 2-4, depending on hunger and financial straits.

Celia Franca
former Artistic Director
National Ballet Company

Annette's Meatloaf

½ cup (125 mL) bread crumbs
1 (1) Medium onion, finely
    chopped
1 tsp. (5 mL) salt
½ tsp. (125 mL) pepper, ground
1 tsp. (5 mL) garlic powder
1 tsp. (5 mL) Bouquet herbes de
    provence
¾ cup (175 mL) water
½ (½) shot glass brandy
1½ lbs. (750 g) ground beef (lean)
1 (1) egg
½ cup (125 mL) slivered almonds

In a bowl mix bread crumbs, onion, salt, pepper, garlic powder and herbes de provence. Add water and brandy. Mix and let stand for 2 minutes. Add the ground beef, mix well, then add the egg.

Shape loaf on a flat baking dish, cover with almonds which should be gently pressed into the loaf. Put 2 strips of bacon over the top, lengthwise, and 1 strip of bacon across.

Bake in a preheated oven at 350°F (180°C) for 45 minutes — 1 hour (depending on how well-done you want the meat loaf). Espagnole Sauce, page 64 is a flavorful addition to this meat loaf.

Serve with stir-fried broccoli and baked potatoes.

**Red wine and candlelight a must!
Serves 4-6.

Annette Av Paul
Les Grands Ballets Canadiens

Annette Av Paul

Born in Stockholm, Sweden, Annette Av Paul received her early training from her mother, a specialist in Dalcroze-type movement classes for children. A graduate of the Royal Opera House, she performed with The Opera Ballet and The Royal Swedish Ballet from 1962 to 1972.

Annette is married to Brian Macdonald who is director of Les Grands Ballets Canadiens.

Penne alla Rubiatta

Dawn Pyke

Dawn Pyke graduated from the Canadian College of dance at Ryerson in 1979. Prior to joining the Alberta Ballet Company for the 1982/3 season, Ms. Pyke was a professional member of Ballet Y's and Studio 103 in Toronto. She moved to Montreal to pursue further study at L'Ecole Superieure De Danse in Quebec, under the direction of Madam Ludmilla Chiriaeff, founder of Les Grands Ballets Canadiens.

A great recipe for a party when you are on a restricted budget, delicious and inexpensive.

4 tbsp. (50 mL) olive oil
4-6 (4-6) large cloves of garlic
3 (3) whole dried chili peppers (less if preferred)
2 x 28 oz. (2 x 796 mL) tins of plum tomatoes
1 lb. (500 g) penne noodles coarsely chopped fresh parsley

Heat the olive oil in a heavy saucepan over a medium heat. Slash garlic cloves and add to warm oil with chili peppers. Sauté until garlic cloves turn brown. Add tomatoes to mixture, breaking them apart with a wooden spoon, but still leaving them chunky.

Simmer sauce for 20-25 minutes.

According to the package directions, take the required amount of penne and cook until al dente (soft).

Drain the noodles well, and stir in the sauce. Let stand for approximately 1 minute. Stir again. Sprinkle with parsley and serve. Also tasty when served cold.

*The amount of garlic recommended may seem excessive but, in fact, is just right.

Serves 4-6.

Dawn Pyke
Dancer
Alberta Ballet Company

Yogurt Omelette

3-4 (3-4) large eggs
4 heaping tbsp. (60mL) of yogurt
    (for delightful variety use
      vanilla, lemon or fruit-
      flavored yogurt)
3 oz. (85g) Camembert cheese,
    thinly sliced
3 tbsp. (45mL) vegetable,
    safflower or peanut oil
½ cup (125 mL) sliced mushrooms
1 (1) tomato, sliced (or your
    favorite vegetables)
½ tsp. (2 mL) salt
¼ tsp. (1 mL) pepper

Mix eggs and yogurt — whip with fork until well blended.

Heat oil in 10'' (25 cm) skillet.

Pour eggs and yogurt mixture into skillet and cover.

When omelette is almost firm, add mushrooms, tomato and then cheese and re-cover until done.

Salt and pepper to taste.

Omelette should be extremely light and should fold easily and slide onto serving plate.

Serves 2.

Mark Lanham
Principal Dancer
Royal Winnipeg Ballet

Mark Lanham

Born in Texas, Mark only began his formal training at the age of 18 years, with Neil and Camille Hess in Amarillo.

In 1975, he received a full scholarship to Ballet West's summer school in Aspen, after which he was taken into the company of Ballet West. There he rose to the rank of Principal dancer and in 1978, with his partner Stacey Swaner, competed in the Second International Ballet Concours in Tokyo, Japan; they were awarded Bronze Medals.

In the fall of 1980, Mark accepted a position as a principal dancer with San Francisco Ballet. In the fall of 1983, he toured throughout the U.S. with Leonid and Valentina Koslov. He joined the RWB in July, 1984.

Desserts

Karen Kain Chantilly

8 (8) egg whites
¼ tsp. (1 mL) cream of tartar
2 cups (500 mL) sugar
1 tsp. (5 mL) vanilla
1½ qts. (1.5 L) sliced strawberries
¼ cup (50 mL) sugar
1 cup (250 mL) whipping cream
2 tbsp. (25 mL) icing sugar
3 tsp. (15 mL) kirsch OR
1 tsp. (5 mL) vanilla

Beat egg whites and cream of tartar until soft peaks form. Gradually beat in sugar, then vanilla, until stiff peaks form. Line a baking sheet with greased foil. Shape meringue into rings 3" wide x 4" high (7 cm x 10 cm) using a piping bag or 2 spoons. Bake 250°F (120°C) until set, 1 to 1½ hours. Turn off oven and let stand 1 hour more. May be stored up to 1 month in freezer. Do not thaw before filling. Makes about 25 meringues.

To make filling, combine strawberries and sugar. Whip cream, gradually adding icing sugar then kirsh or vanilla. Fill each meringue with ¼ cup (50 mL) strawberry mixture and 2 tbsp. (25 mL) whipped cream. Garnish with strawberry slice. May stand up to 1 hour at room temperature before serving. Fresh seasonal fruit may be substituted for strawberries.
25 servings.

Karen Kain
Principal Dancer
The National Ballet of Canada

See photograph page 80.

Karen Kain:

Born in Hamilton, Ontario, Karen Kain trained at the National Ballet School of Canada with Betty Oliphant. She has performed with the company since 1969. Known for her performances in the 19th century classics, she has taken the principal roles in Frederick Ashton's production of "La Fille Mal Gardee" Erik Bruhn's "Swan Lake" and the company productions of "Giselle" and 'Sleeping Beauty."

Her appearances in these roles with Rudolf Nureyev in his New York season have made her well known and acclaimed throughout the dance world

Pavlova

A beautiful light desert.

3 (3) egg whites
4 tbsp. (60 mL) cold water
1¼ cups (300 mL) castor or berry sugar
4 tsp. (20 mL) cornstarch
⅛ tsp. (0.5 mL) salt
½ tsp. (2 mL) vanilla
1 tsp. (5 mL) vinegar
1 cup (250 mL) whipping cream
fruit in season, e.g. bananas, peaches,
kiwifruit, apricots, etc.

Beat egg whites until very stiff, then add water, beating all the while. Gradually beat in sugar, ¼ cup (50 mL) at a time. Add cornstarch, salt, vanilla and vinegar. Place dampened grease-proof paper on top of cookie sheet and then pile mixture onto tray, forming a 10" (25 cm) circle with a slight hollow in the middle. Bake for 1 hour at 350°F. Remove from the oven and allow to cool. Place a large serving plate carefully on top of the pavlova and turn cookie sheet over until it is on top. Gently peel off wax paper. Whip the cream until thick and spread evenly over the pavlova. Decorate with fruit of your choice and serve immediately. Serves 10-12.

Coral Luscombe

Vacherin Norma

3 (3) egg whites
6 oz. (170 g) soft brown sugar
1 cup (250 mL) whipping cream, whipped
3 oz. (85 g) crystallized ginger, chopped
1 tsp. (5 mL) finely ground coffee powder

Whisk egg whites until very stiff. Whisk in 1 oz. (25 g) sugar and then fold in the remaining sugar.

Divide mixture between 2 prepared, buttered and floured, 8" (20 cm) diameter cake pans. Bake at 250°F (120°C) for 2 hours or until firm.

3 hours before serving fill with whipped cream into which has been mixed the chopped crystallized ginger and coffee powder. Serves 6.

Shelagh Aizlewood

Coffee Pudding

So easy, but a lovely, rich, creamy taste.

½ lb. (250 g) marshmallows (large)
½ cup (125 mL) strong hot coffee
⅛ tsp. (0.5 mL) salt
1 tsp. (5 mL) vanilla
1 cup (250 mL) whipping cream

Melt the marshmallows in coffee. Add salt and vanilla. Whip cream until stiff and add to cooled marshmallow mixture. Pour into serving dishes and chill until set.
Serves 6.

Heather Baker
President
Alberta Ballet Guild, Calgary

Chocolate Chestnut Mousse

A delicious rich dessert for a special occasion.

6 oz. (175 g) dark cooking chocolate
3 tbsp. (45 mL) butter
3 tbsp. (45 mL) fine granulated sugar
15 oz. (425 g) can chestnut purée
3 tbsp. (45 mL) rum or brandy
1 cup (250 mL) whipping cream
whole sweetened chestnuts (marrons glacé)
whipping cream, whipped
grated chocolate

Put chocolate pieces into a small bowl and stand over a pan of simmering water to melt.

Cream butter and sugar together. Add chestnut purée and mix thoroughly.

Add melted chocolate, then rum or brandy, and lastly the un-whipped cream. Pour into a 4-cup (1 L) serving dish.

Decorate with whole sweetened chestnuts (marrons glacé) or whipped cream, and sprinkle with grated chocolate.
Serves 6-8 or more!

Caroline de L. Davies

Lime Raspberry Trifle

A delicious, refreshing dessert, perfect for a buffet supper!

2	lb. (1 kg) raspberries
8	oz. (250 g) icing sugar
2	(2) packets trifle sponge cakes (4 cakes)
⅔	cup (150 mL) medium-sweet white wine
½	cup (125 mL) Framboise (raspberry liqueur)

Custard

2	cups (500 mL) milk
2	cups (500 mL) half & half
3	tsp. (15 mL) cornflour
3	oz. (75 g) castor or berry sugar
10	(10) eggs

Topping

1	tbsp. (15 mL) grated rind of limes
4	cups (1 L) whipping cream, whipped
4	tbsp. (50 mL) medium sherry
4	(4) limes, thinly sliced

Put raspberries and icing sugar into saucepan, heat gently until juice runs. Stir to dissolve sugar then bring to the boil. Rub fruit through sieve, cool. Add more icing sugar, if necessary, to taste. Bring milk and cream to boil. Mix together cornflour and sugar, gradually beat in eggs. Pour over the boiling milk mixture, stirring constantly. Return custard to pan, stir over a low heat for about 10 minutes, until thickened. Remove from heat, leave to cool.

Sandwich sponges together with cooled Raspberry purée. Arrange over bottom of two 6 cup (1.5 L) serving bowls. Mix together the white wine and liqueur, pour it over the sponge cakes and level the top. Leave overnight to cool completely.

Stir the lime rind into the whipped cream and gradually stir in the sherry. Spread the cream over the custard, reserving a little for decoration. Pipe rosettes around edges. Halve lime slices, twist and arrange on cream. Chill before serving.
Serves 24.

Shelagh Aizlewood

Raspberry Pudding

Nadine Baylis

Nadine Baylis trained at the Central School of Art in London, England. She has become an internationally acclaimed designer in the Theatre, Opera, Ballet and Musical Theatre.

Her work includes designs for Rudolf Nureyev and Glen Tetley. Her production designs are included in such well known companies as Ballet Rambert, The Royal Ballet, The Australian Ballet and The American Ballet Theatre.

She has created designs for the Edinburgh Festival and the Royal Shakespearean Company, the Royal Opera House, Covent Garden and The Paris Opera.

Her recent works include the sets and costumes for the Alberta Ballet Company's production of Coppelia.

Simple but sensational, this dessert is for those who don't have to watch the calories.

1½ lb. (700 g) raspberries, fresh or frozen
2 cups (500 mL) whipping cream
sugar to taste (white)
brown sugar for topping

Wash and dry the raspberries and place in a large shallow baking dish. Add sugar to taste.

Beat the cream until thick and spread evenly over the raspberries, covering them completely, ensuring that the edges are sealed.

Refrigerate for an hour or freeze for a short time.

Cover the cream with a thin even layer of brown sugar. Preheat the broiler until red hot. Stand the dish on a flat baking tray, place under the broiler just long enough for the sugar to melt and bubble but not burn.

Refrigerate again until ready to serve.

Serve with small almond biscuits.

* Marks & Spencers have excellent frozen raspberries all year round.

Serves: 4 - 8.

Nadine Baylis
Set and Costume Deigner
Alberta Ballet Company

See photograph page 96.

"Temps-levé" aux Fruits

Dessert pour danseurs (Dancer's dessert).

1 lb. (500 g) plums
1¼ cups (300 mL) milk
4 (4) eggs
½ cup (125 mL) sugar
1 tsp. (5 mL) salt
1 cup (250 mL) flour
½ tsp. (2 mL) baking powder*
1½ tbsp. (20 mL) melted butter
¼ cup (50 mL) confectioner's
    sugar

Remove pits from the plums, and place in an 8-cup (2 L) baking dish.

Combine remaining ingredients, except the confectioner's sugar, in a blender.

Blend until smooth.

Pour batter over the plums and bake 30 minutes in a 350°F (180°C) oven.

Dust surface with sifted confectioner's sugar and serve hot.

This dessert can be made with cherries, peaches, apples or other fruits in season.

It is particulary good served with whipped cream.

Serves 6.

Ludmilla Chiriaeff
Founder
Les Grands Ballets Canadiens

*baking powder is necessary only in Alberta because of altitude.

Madame Ludmilla Chiriaeff

Madame Chiriaeff was raised in Berlin where she studied with Mikhail Fokine and Alexandra Nicolaieva.

She performed with the Ballet Russe de Monte Carlo while continuing her training in Paris, and in the early 1950's emigrated to Canada to form Les Ballets Chiriaeff, later known as Les Grands Ballets Canadiens.

While creating a large repertory for the Company and training its dancers, she found time to choreograph short ballets for the French-language Canadian Broadcasting Corporation.

Madame Chiriaeff has received the Order of Canada for her services to the world of dance.

Austrian Pancake

A very tasty recipe which can be served as a dessert or a brunch dish.

Svea Eklof

"exquisite classical technique and musicality. . ."
Hamilton Spectator, March, 1984.
Currently in her second season with the Royal Winnipeg Ballet, Svea previously performed in Europe and North America with the Pennsylvania Ballet Company, the Ballet Classico de Mexico, the Ballet du Grand Theatre du Geneva, the Nederlans Dans Theatre, the North Carolina Dance Theatre and the Alberta Ballet (Principal Dancer).

Svea has worked with a number of eminent teachers, among them, Laura Alonso, Madam Alexandra Danilova and the late George Balanchine.

1	cup (250 mL) all-purpose flour
2-3	tbsp. (25-45 mL) sugar
¾	tsp. (4mL) salt
3	(3) eggs
2	cups (500 mL) milk
1	cup (250 mL) light cream (half and half)
2	tbsp. (25 mL) butter
2	tbsp. (25 mL) confectioner's sugar
1	cup (250 mL) apricot preserves
1-2	tbsp. (15-25 mL) apricot brandy (optional)

Pre-heat oven to 375°F (190°C).

Sift flour, sugar, salt together into a bowl.

With fork beat the eggs in a medium bowl; beat in milk and cream until well mixed.

Stir into flour mixture; mix until smooth.

Meanwhile in a heavy 10" (25 cm) skillet heat butter until sizzling.

Turn batter into skillet; bake 30 minutes or until set and golden on top (this will rise!)

Sprinkle with confectioner's sugar and serve with apricot preserves mixed with brandy (optional). Serve in wedges.
Serves 4-6.

Svea Eklof
Principal Dancer
Royal Winnipeg Ballet

Strawberry Cream Cheese Torte

9" (23 cm) baked pie shell

Filling

4 oz. (125 g) cream cheese, softened
¼ cup (50 mL) light brown sugar
½ tsp. (2 mL) vanilla
½ tsp. (2 mL) lemon juice
½ cup (125 mL) whipping cream, whipped

Glaze

⅓ cup (75 mL) light brown sugar
2 tbsp. (25 mL) cornstarch
½ cup (125 mL) water
⅓ cup (75 mL) grenadine syrup
½ tsp. (2 mL) lemon juice

3 cups (750 mL) fresh strawberries, sliced

Prepare pie shell.

To prepare filling, beat cream cheese, brown sugar, vanilla and lemon juice until smooth and creamy. Fold in the whipped cream. Spread evenly over bottom of cooled pie shell. Chill 1 hour.

To prepare glaze, mix brown sugar and cornstarch in a saucepan. Slowly stir in water. Add grenadine and lemon juice. Cook, stirring constantly, until thickened and clear. Cool.

Arrange strawberries in overlapping pattern from outside of pastry shell to center on cool cream cheese filling. With pastry brush generously cover strawberries with glaze. Chill 2 to 3 hours to set glaze.
Serves 6.

Betty Afaganis

Semisweet Strawberry Cream Pie

1½ cups (375 mL) chocolate wafer crumbs
6 tbsp. (90 mL) melted butter
2 tbsp. (25 mL) sugar
⅓ cup (75 mL) sugar
⅛ tsp. (0.5 mL) salt
¼ cup (50 mL) cornstarch
¼ cup (50 mL) cold milk
2 cups (500 mL) scalded milk
1 oz. (30 g) unsweetened chocolate
8 oz. (250 g) pkg. cream cheese, softened
6-8 oz. (175-250 g) fresh sliced strawberries
1 cup (250 mL) whipping cream whipped &
sweetened to taste

Combine chocolate wafer, butter and 2 tbsp. (25 mL) sugar. Press into 9'' (23 cm) pie plate. Chill until filling is ready. Mix sugar, salt and cornstarch with ¼ cup (50 mL) cold milk. Add a small amount of the scalded milk, stir well and return entire mixture to pot containing remainder of warm milk. Melt the chocolate and add to milk mixture and cook over low heat stirring constantly until mixture boils and thickens. Cover and simmer very slowly (or in double boiler) for 20-30 minutes, stirring occasionally.

Cool to lukewarm and beat in cream cheese until smooth. Pour into pie shell and refrigerate for about 3 hours. Top with sliced strawberries and whipped cream, and refrigerate for a further 2 hours. Seasonal fresh fruit may be substitued for strawberries. Serves 6-8.

Michelle Martin
Former Dancer
Alberta Ballet Company

Crêpes De Fruits Flambé À L'Amaretto Et Grand Marnier

1 cup (250 mL) flour, sifted
¼ tsp. (1 mL) salt
5 (5) eggs
1¼ cups (300 mL) milk
3 tbsp. (45 mL) melted butter
   **fruit - anything you like.
   Suggestions: 1 apple, 3
   bananas, 3 kiwi, 2 pears, 12
   strawberries, and 2
   nectarines.
2 tbsp. (25 mL) brown sugar
   juice from 1 (1) lemon
½ cup (125 mL) of fresh orange
   juice
2 oz. (50 mL) Amaretto
2 oz. (50 mL) Grand Marnier
½ cup (125 mL) grated cheese
   (medium strong - e.g. Gouda)
   vanilla ice cream or whipped
   cream for topping (optional)

Claude Caron

A native of Northern Quebec, Claude Caron received his dance training at the Eddy Toussaint Dance School and les Grands Ballets Canadiens. He has toured extensively throughout Eastern Canada, Mexico, Martinique and Guadeloupe. While a member of Eddy Toussaint. Caron appeared in several television specials including CBC's Inauguration of LG2. He joined the Alberta Ballet Company in 1982, and the staff of the Alberta Ballet School in 1984 as guest instructor teaching jazz dance.

Mix flour and salt in 1 bowl. In separate bowl beat eggs along with half of the milk and all of the butter. Pour this mixture into the flour, stirring, and add the rest of the milk. Mix well by stirring until smooth (like a thin pancake mixture)

Put in the refrigerator while preparing the fruit and pour yourself a nice glass of "French Wine."

Peel the fruit and slice into quarter-moon-shaped slices. Mix fruit in a bowl and sprinkle brown sugar on top. Pour lemon juice over it.

*It is now probably time to pour yourself another glass of wine - go for it!! Put fruit into refrigerator.

Crêpes De Fruits Flambé Á L'Amaretto Et Grand Marnier (cont'd.)

Use a 9" (23 cm) coated frying pan or crêpe pan. Pour enough of the batter into the pan to thinly cover the botton of the pan entirely. Cook on either side until the crêpe is a very light brown color.

Continue until all the batter has been used - approximately 8 - 10 crêpes. Put crêpes aside. They may be made ahead, layered with waxed paper and reheated when ready to use.

Cook all the fruit and orange juice in a frying pan over a moderate heat for 5-10 minutes. Pour Amaretto and Grand Marnier over fruit mixture. *Turn off burner*. Let the fruit sit for 30 seconds. Turn out light and flambé for 30 seconds. cover with lid to put out the flames (before all the alchohol is burned off).

To fill crêpes, place a generous helping of fruit in the centre of each crêpe. Fold in half and in half again. Pour some of the syrup over the top. Sprinkle with cheese. Serve hot. Great topped with vanilla ice cram or whipped cream and served with a bottle of French white wine!

Bon Appetit!
Serves 4-5.

Claude Caron
Male Soloist
Alberta Ballet Company

See photograph page 80.

Sour Cream Lemon Pie

9" (23 cm) baked pie shell
1 cup (250 mL) granulated sugar
3 tbsp. (50 mL) cornstarch
1 tbsp. (15 mL) all-purpose flour
1 tbsp. (15 mL) grated lemon peel
⅓ cup (75 mL) fresh lemon juice
1 cup (250 mL) light cream
¼ cup (50 mL) butter
1 cup (250 mL) sour cream

Sour Cream Topping

1 cup (250 mL) whipping cream
2 tbsp. (25 mL) icing sugar
½ cup (125 mL) sour cream
½ tsp. (2 mL) almond extract
grated lemon peel
lemon slices

Have pie shell ready. In a saucepan over medium heat, combine sugar, cornstarch, flour, lemon peel, lemon juice and light cream. Bring slowly to boil, stirring constantly with wire whisk. Add butter and cook until thick and smooth. Remove from the heat and let cool. Stir in sour cream and pour filling into baked pie shell. Refrigerate, covered, until ready to serve.

Sour Cream Topping

Whip cream and fold in sugar, sour cream and almond extract. Spoon over lemon filling. Sprinkle with grated lemon peel and garnish with lemon slices.
Serves 6-8.

Marilyn Millar
Vice-President Board of Directors
Alberta Ballet Company

Broken Glass Pie

A colorful dessert, ideal for a children's party.

Filling

        3 oz. (85 g) pkg. red Jell-o
        3 oz. (85 g) pkg. lime Jell-o
        3 oz. (85 g) pkg. lemon Jell-o
    1½ cups (375 mL) hot water
        2 cups (500 mL) whipping cream
        2 tbsp. (25 mL) sugar
        1 tbsp. (7 g) envelope of plain gelatin
      ½ cup (125 mL) cold water
      ½ cup (125 mL) hot water
      ¼ cup (50 mL) pineapple juice

Pie Shell

      ⅓ cup (75 mL) butter
      ⅓ cup (75 mL) sugar
        1 tsp. (5 mL) cinnamon
        1 cup (250 mL) graham cracker crumbs

Melt the butter and add the sugar, cinnamon and crumbs. Press into an 8" (20 cm) pie dish and chill.

Dissolve each packet of Jell-o in ½ cup (125 mL) of hot water. Pour into separate pie pans and chill until set. Whip cream with the sugar. Dissolve the gelatin in ½ cup (125 mL) of cold water, then add half a cup of hot water. Add the gelatin mixture and pineapple juice to whipped cream and mix well. Cut the Jell-o into cubes, add to cream mixture and mix well.

Pour into chilled pie shell and refrigerate until ready to serve. Serves 6-8.

Charlotte Williams

Fantastic Frozen Peanut Butter Pie

A lovely creamy dessert with a subtle peanut flavor.

9" (23 cm) baked graham cracker crust
8 oz. (250 g) cream cheese, at room temperature
1 cup (250 mL) unsifted powdered sugar
½ cup (125 mL) peanut butter, at room temperature
½ cup (125 mL) milk
1 tsp. (5 mL) vanilla
3 cups (750 mL) whipped topping
OR
1½ cups (375 mL) whipping cream, sweetened and whipped
¼ cup (50 mL) chopped peanuts

Have pie crust ready. Beat cream cheese until fluffy. Add sugar gradually, beating until smooth. Add peanut butter, mixing well. Stir in milk gradually. Add vanilla. Fold whipped topping or whipped cream into mixture with rubber scraper or whisk. Pour into cooled crust. Sprinkle with chopped peanuts. Freeze at least 4 hours. Let sit for 20 minutes before cutting.
Serves 6-8.

Marilyn Millar
Vice-President Board of Directors
Alberta Ballet Company

Sex in a Pan

Evelyn Hart

"Miss Hart is a gem. Her body and its placement are perfect, and she moves with a sort of grave, objective self-absorption as if she was simply the instrument of dance. . .she has the ineffable image of greatness about her." Clive Barnes, New York Post.

Hart began training at the Dorothy Carter School of Dance Arts in London, Ontario. After a brief stint with the National Ballet School, she came to Winnipeg in 1973. She is the RWB's leading light, dancing principal roles in virtually the entire repertoire.

Hart has performed tour throughout North America and in Greece, Cyprus, England, Ireland, West Germany and Egypt.

In 1983, she was made an Officer of the Order of Canada.

2 cups (500 mL) graham wafer crumbs
½ cup (125 mL) butter, melted
1 cup (250 mL) butter
2 cups (500 mL) icing sugar
3 (3) eggs
1 cup (250 mL) semisweet chocolate chips
½ cup (125 mL) cup cocoa
2-4 tbsp. (25-50 mL) liqueur, your favorite (optional)
1 cup (250 mL) whipping cream, whipped

Line a 9" x 13" (23 cm x 33 cm) pan with a graham wafer crust made by combining graham wafer crumbs and melted butter.

Melt chocolate.

Whip unmelted butter and add the icing sugar bit by bit until thoroughly mixed and fluffy.

Add eggs 1 at a time and beat well after each addition.

Add melted chocolate and mix thoroughly.

Add liqueur, if using.

Pour into pan and top with whipped cream.

Chill overnight. For a more elegant presentation, this could be made in 2, 9" (23 cm) round pans and served in wedges.

Serves 8-10.

Evelyn Hart
Principal Dancer
Royal Winnipeg Ballet

Frozen Strawberry Cream

Topping

    ½ cup (125 mL) butter
    ¼ cup (50 mL) brown sugar
    1 cup (250 mL) flour
    ½ cup (125 mL) walnuts

Filling

    11 oz. (310 g) package frozen strawberries
    1 tbsp. (15 mL) lemon juice
    1 tsp. (5 mL) vanilla
    1 cup (250 mL) sugar
    2 (2) egg whites
    1 cup (250 mL) whipping cream

Combine topping ingredients lightly. Place in pan and bake at 400°F (200°C), stirring occasionally until brown, about 15 minutes. Cool. Press half the mixture into the bottom of a 9" x 13" (23 x 33 cm) pan. Leave half for top.

Place all filling ingredients except whipping cream into a large bowl. Beat for 20 minutes with an electric beater. Fold in whipped whipping cream. Pour over mixture in pan. Top with remaining crust. Freeze for at least 8 hours. Cut into squares.
*In covered pan, this dessert can remain in the freezer for several weeks.
Serves 12-14.

Dr. H. J. Shimizu

Nancy's Favorite Cheesecake

Nancy Shainberg

Nancy Shainberg came to the Alberta Ballet Company from Memphis, Tennessee. Following a summer with the School of American Ballet in New York, she went on to complete her training at the National Academy of Dance. In 1976, she joined the North Carolina Dance Theatre, and in 1980 the Alberta Ballet Company. She was promoted to principal for the 1984-85 season. Shainberg was invited in 1984 to perform in New York at the Riverside Church Festival opening gala, where she received critical acclaim. She has now retired from dance, and lives with her husband in the United States.

'12 ozs. (340 g) cream cheese, softened
2 (2) eggs, beaten
½ cup (125 mL) sugar
8" (20 cm) graham cracker crust
1½ tsp. (7 mL) sugar
1 tsp. (5 mL) vanilla
1 cup (250 mL) sour cream

Preheat oven to 350°F (180°C). Cream softened cream cheese well. Add beaten eggs and sugar to mixture and continue beating well. Pour mixture into graham cracker crust and bake for 25-30 minutes. Let cool.

For topping combine sugar, vanilla and sour cream. Mix by hand. Spread (do not pour) topping on. Cool and refrigerate several hours before serving. Garnish with fresh fruit in season.

Delicious!

Serves 4-6.

Nancy Shainberg
Former Principal Dancer
Alberta Ballet Company

Chocolate Amaretto Cheesecake

A must for cheesecake lovers.

Crust

¼ cups (300 mL) chocolate wafer crumbs
2 tbsp. (25 mL) sugar
¼ cup (50 mL) melted butter

Filling

16 oz. (500 g) cream cheese
½ cup (125 mL) granulated sugar
2 (2) large eggs
¾ cup (175 mL) melted semisweet chocolate, cooled
½ tsp. (5 mL) almond flavoring
1 tsp. (5 mL) vanilla
⅓ cup (75 mL) amaretto
⅔ cup (150 mL) sour cream

Topping

¼ cup (50 mL) semisweet chocolate
1 tsp. (5 mL) shortening

Combine crumbs, sugar and butter. Press into the bottom and halfway up the sides of a buttered 7''-8'' (18-20 cm) springform pan. Chill while making filling. Beat cream cheese well until smooth. Beat in sugar gradually. Beat in eggs 1 at a time at low speed. Add cooled chocolate, flavorings, amaretto and sour cream. Beat at low speed until thoroughly blended. Pour into prepared pan.

Bake at 300°F (150°C) for 1 hour. Turn off heat and leave cake in oven for further hour. Cool in pan at room temperature then chill at least 24 hours in refrigerator.

For topping, melt chocolate with shortening. Spread over top of the cheesecake. Can be garnished or served with whipped cream flavored with amaretto if desired.
Serves 8.

Shelagh Aizlewood

Diana's Chocolate Brandy Cake

8 oz. (250 g) digestive biscuits
8 oz. (250 g) unsalted butter
8 oz. (250 g) dark chocolate
2 (2) eggs
3 oz. (85 g) sugar
2 tbsp. (25 mL) brandy
4 oz. (115 g) glacé cherries
4 oz. (115 g) chopped walnuts
1 cup (250 mL) whipping cream, whipped

Crush digestive biscuits with a rolling pin. Melt the butter and chocolate over a low heat.

Beat together the eggs and sugar until light and fluffy, and add to the chocolate mixture. Add the digestive biscuits, brandy and ¾ of the cherries and walnuts. Mix together and pour into a 6'' (15 cm) cake tin with removable base. Leave to set for several hours in the refrigerator. Decorate the top with remaining cherries and walnuts. Just before serving, decorate with piped whipped cream.

**This cake is very rich so a little goes a long way. It freezes well.
Serves 8-10.

Caroline de L. Davies

See photograph page 80.

Chocolate Zucchini Cake

A rich and attractive-looking cake with a delicious creamy icing.

3 x 1 oz. (3 x 30 g) squares unsweetened chocolate
3 cups (750 mL) flour
1½ tsp. (7 mL) baking powder
1 tsp. (5 mL) baking soda
1 tsp. (5 mL) salt
4 (4) eggs
3 cups (750 mL) sugar
1½ cups (375 mL) salad oil (not olive oil)
3 cups (750 mL) grated zucchini
1 cup (250 mL) chopped nuts

Preheat oven to 350°F (180°C).
Grease and flour a 10" (25 cm) tube pan.
Melt chocolate over hot water, let cool.
Sift together flour, baking powder, baking soda, salt. Set aside.
Beat eggs until thick, add sugar ¼ cup (50 mL) at a time and beat until smooth. To egg mixture add salad oil and chocolate and beat until blended.
Add dry ingredients, mixing until smooth. Add zucchini and nuts.
Bake for 1¼ hours or until cooked right through. Cool for 15 minutes before removing from pan.
Dust with powdered sugar or frost with Cream Cheese Frosting. This cake freezes well.

Cream Cheese Frosting

6 oz. (170 g) cream cheese, softened
1 lb. (500 g) icing sugar
2 tsp. (10 mL) orange or lemon juice
1 tsp. (5 mL) vanilla or almond extract
1 tsp. (5 mL) grated orange or lemon peel

Beat cheese until light, then slowly add sugar. Thin with juice. Add vanilla and peel. Beat until smooth and creamy.
Serves 10-12.

David La Hay
Principal Dancer
Les Grands Ballets Canadiens

Mexican Chocolate Cake

¼ lb. (115 g) margarine
½ cup (125 mL) vegetable oil
2 oz. (60 g) unsweetened chocolate or 4 tbsp. (60 mL) cocoa
1 cup (250 mL) water
2 cups (500 mL) flour
1 tsp. (5 mL) soda
2 cups (500 mL) sugar
½ cup (125 mL) sour milk (add 1½ tsp. (7 mL) vinegar to ½ cup (125 mL) milk
2 (2) eggs beaten
1 tsp. (5 mL) vanilla
1 tsp. (5 mL) cinnamon

Preheat oven to 350°F (180°C). Combine margarine, oil, chocolate and water in a saucepan and heat until chocolate has melted.

Combine remaining ingredients in a large bowl, add to the chocolate mixture. (This mixture is not thick.) Pour into a greased and floured 12" x 18" (30 cm x 45 cm) cake pan or a jelly roll pan. Bake 20-25 minutes.

** In Alberta add an extra 1½ tbsp. (25 mL) flour and an extra ½ cup (125 mL) of sour milk to cake mixture.

5 minutes before cake is done, prepare the frosting.

Frosting

¼ lb. (115 g) margarine
2 oz. (60 mL) unsweetened chocolate
6 tbsp. (90 mL) milk
16 oz. (500 g) confectioner's sugar
1 tsp. (5 mL) vanilla
½ cup (125 mL) chopped pecans (or walnuts)

Combine margarine, chocolate and milk in a saucepan. Heat until bubbles form around the edges. Remove from heat. Add confectioner's sugar, vanilla, nuts and beat. (Icing is not stiff.) Ice the cake while it is still warm.
Serves 10-20.

Erene Augustyn
(Mrs. Frank Augustyn)

Carrot Cake

A delicious moist cake.

> 1 cup (250 mL) sugar
> 1 cup (250 mL) salad oil
> 4 (4) eggs separated
> 1 cup (250 mL) all-purpose flour
> 1 cup (250 mL) whole-wheat flour
> 1½ tsp. (7 mL) baking soda
> 4 tsp. (20 mL) baking powder
> 1 tsp. (5 mL) salt
> 2 tsp. (10 mL) cinnamon
> 2 cups (500 mL) grated raw carrot
> 1½ cups (375 mL) grated apple**
> 1 cup (250 mL) golden raisins
> ½ cup (125 mL) chopped walnuts

Blend sugar, oil and egg yolks and beat until slightly thickened. Sift dry ingredients and combine with the above ingredients. Add carrots, apple, raisins and nuts. Beat egg whites until stiff and fold into batter. Pour into greased and floured 9" x 13" (23 cm x 33 cm) baking pan. Bake at 350°F (180°C) for 35-40 minutes.

Ice with the following icing.

Icing

> 6 oz. (170 g) cream cheese
> ⅓ cup (75 mL) butter
> 1½ cups (375 mL) icing sugar
> ¾ tsp. (4 mL) vanilla

Whip cream cheese and butter until fluffy. Beat in sugar and vanilla. Spread over carrot cake when cool.

**In season try 1 cup (250 mL) apple and ½ cup (125 mL) grated peaches.

Serves 15-20.

Chip Seibert,
Soloist
Alberta Ballet Company

Chip Seibert

Born in Edmonton, Alberta. Began his Ballet training at the Joliffe Academy of Dance after a long involvement with musical theatre. He later attended the National Ballet School as a special student and graduated from the Quinte Dance Centre in Belleville, Ont. He joined the Alberta Ballet Company for the 1980-81 season. In 1980 he returned to Quinte as a guest artist for a Gala performance. In December 1982 he accepted a contract with the New Zealand Ballet. The year was highlighted by a special Gala performance of Coppelia for their Royal Highnesses Prince Charles and Princess Diana. He returned to the Alberta Ballet Company in January 1984 as a soloist.

Pink Lady Cake

¼ lb. (125 g) butter
1 cup (250 mL) sugar
2 (2) eggs
¾ cup (175 mL) milk
¼ tsp. (1 mL) cochineal or red food coloring
1 cup (250 mL) flour
1 tsp. (5 mL) baking powder
¼ lb. (113.5 g) fine coconut

Grease and flour an 8" (20 cm) square baking pan.
Cream the butter and sugar. Add eggs and beat well. Mix in the milk and cochineal or red food coloring, then the flour, baking powder and coconut. Pour into pan. Bake at 350°F (180°C). For 1 hour.
Serves: 8-10.

Coral Luscombe

Homemade Vanilla

1 vanilla bean
⅓ tsp. (1.5 mL) sugar
3 oz. (100 mL) vodka

Cut vanilla bean into pieces and place it in a glass jar along with sugar and vodka. Cover the jar tightly and let the vanilla bean steep for 1 month. Shake it every day. It will then be ready to use. To make larger quantities, simply double or triple the ingredients.

Caroline de L. Davies

Coppelia

1. Raspberry Pudding   page 77

"Nutcracker" Eggnog

This festive eggnog was served backstage to the A.B.C. dancers at the Christmas 1984 "Nutcracker" performances in Calgary. The dancers adored it and kept coming back for more. They seemed to float effortlessly through the air after a few cups of this elixir and they hinted that this concoction should become part of their Nutcracker tradition!

> 12 (12) eggs
> ¾ cup (175 mL) white sugar
> 1 cup (250 mL) rum
> 2 cups (500 mL) whisky
> 4 cups (1 L) whipping cream
> 2 qts. (2 L) commercial eggnog
> grated nutmeg

Separate egg yolks from whites. Put yolks in large bowl and beat, gradually adding sugar while beating. Gradually add rum and whisky, beating all the time.** In a separate bowl whip cream until stiff (peaks will stand up). Fold cream into the rum mixture. Lastly, beat egg whites until stiff. Fold into the mixture. Add carton of ready-made eggnog slowly. Serve at once sprinkled with nutmeg in a large bowl.

**The yolk and liquor mixture can be made ahead of time and kept in the refrigerator frozen and thawed when required. Add cream and egg whites just before serving. This recipe may be halved.

Serves 10-20. [22 cups (6L)]

Susannah Hamer
Alberta Ballet Guild, Calgary

Annette's Black Currant Schnapps

The hardest part is to find the black currants. It is well worth growing a bush yourself. The result cures any cold and does lift your spirits on a dark November evening. This is a Swedish favorite.

    black currants
1 tsp. (5 mL) sugar
    vodka

Fill any size bottle ¾ full with fresh or frozen black currants. Add sugar and fill the bottle to the top with vodka of your choice. Keep in the refrigerator for 6-8 weeks.

Taste the clear red drink in small schnapps glasses. The berries are tart and can be eaten, but can also be re-used, vodka added, *NOT MORE SUGAR.* Crush berries gently with wooden handle. Keep in the refrigerator for 3 more weeks. Can be made to last most of the winter.

Annette Av Paul
Former Principal Dancer
Les Grands Ballets Canadiens

See photograph page 80.

Russian Jam

Nadia Potts

Nadia Potts was born in England and came to Canada when she was 4. At 7 she began studying with Betty Oliphant at the National Ballet School when it opened in 1959. She graduated in 1966 and joined the National Ballet.

She has danced Nutcracker with Fernando Bujones, Four Schumann Pieces with Rudolf Nureyev and Swan Lake with Mikhail Baryshnikov in his debut in the ballet.

In 1970 Potts won the bronze medal at the International Ballet Competition in Varna and with Clinton Rothwell won the prize for the best Pas De Deux.

Potts has also taught ballet at the Dance Centre/Les Ballets Jazz in Toronto, the National Ballet School and George Brown College.

An easy method for making tasty colorful fruit jams.

Any fresh fruit in season: strawberries, peaches, plums, apricots or cherries.
White sugar

In a large saucepan put 1 cup (250 mL) of sugar to 1 cup (250 mL) of pitted and cut up fruit. Strawberries and cherries can be left whole.

Bring to the boil and simmer for a couple of hours. Skim off foam as the jam cooks.

The jam is ready when it has thickened. Test it by pouring a little on a plate and allowing it to cool, (This jam tends to be slightly runny).

Pour into clean jam jars and put the lids on. The jam lasts for a few years without refrigeration or a wax cover.

If the jam starts to crystallize, reheat.

Nadia Potts
Principal Dancer
The National Ballet Company

Russian Toffee

A delicious chewy toffee with a rich caramel flavor.

½ **lb. (250 g) sweet butter**
10 **oz. (300 mL) tin Borden's Eagle Brand**
   sweetened condensed milk
2 **cups (500 mL) brown sugar**
1 **cup (250 mL) corn syrup**

In a heavy saucepan melt the butter. Add the condensed milk and syrup, stirring constantly with a wooden spoon. Add the sugar. Bring to the boil and cook for 20-30 minutes, stirring constantly at 235°F (115°C) on a candy thermometer (soft-ball stage). Pour into a greased 10" x 10" (25 x 25 cm) cake pan and allow to cool. Cut into small rectangular pieces and wrap in wax paper. Serves 8-10.

Nadia Potts
Principal Dancer
The National Ballet Company

Notes

Imperial Measure Equivalents

(All measurements are level)

Table of Equivalents

1 cup (8 fluid ozs.)	— 16 tablespoons
¾ cup (6 fl. ozs.)	— 12 tablespoons
⅔ cup (5⅓ fl. ozs.)	— 10 tablespoons, plus 2 teaspoons
½ cup (4 fl. ozs.)	— 8 tablespoons
⅓ cup (2⅔ fl. ozs.)	— 5 tablespoons, plus 1 teaspoon
¼ cup (2 fl. ozs.)	— 4 tablespoons
⅛ cup (1 fl. oz.)	— 2 tablespoons
1 tablespoon (½ fl. oz.)	— 3 teaspoons

If you have to convert weights to measures in a recipe this table will help you:

Food	Weight of 1 Cup	Measure in Ounces
Butter	8 oz.	1 oz. — 2 tbsp.
Cocoa	4½ oz.	1 oz. — 3½ tbsp.
Cornstarch		1 oz. — 3½ tbsp.
Gelatin		1 oz. — 3 tbsp.
Flour (all-purpose, sifted)	4½ oz.	8 oz. — 1⅞ cups
Sugar (brown, packed)	7 oz.	8 oz. — 1⅛ cups
Sugar (granulated)	7 oz.	8 oz. — 1⅛ cups
Sugar (icing) (sifted)	4½ oz	8 oz. — 2 cups
Shortening	7 oz.	8 oz. — 1⅛ cups

Imperial Measure Equivalents
(All measurements are level)

Table of Equivalents

1 gallon (160 fl. oz.)	— 4 quarts
1 quart (40 fl. oz.)	— 5 cups
1 pint (20 fl. oz.)	— 2½ cups

Estimating Raw Ingredients

Macaroni	1 cup uncooked	— 3 cups cooked
Rice	1 cup uncooked	— 3 cups cooked
	1 cup precooked	— 2 cups cooked
Icing Sugar	1 lb.	— 3-4 cups sifted
Brown Sugar	1 lb.	— 2¼ cups sifted
Granulated Sugar	1 lb.	— 2½ cups
Heavy Cream	1 cup	— 2 cups whipped
Cheese	1 lb.	— 4 cups grated
Egg Whites	1 cup	— 8 egg whites

Metric Conversion
Canadian Home Economics Association

When translating recipes to metric, and where possible replace:

⅛ teaspoon or a dash with 1 mL		3 tablespoons	50 mL
OR, Pepper, to taste		¼ cup	50 mL
¼ teaspoon	1 mL	⅓ cup	75 mL
½ teaspoon	2 mL	½ cup	125 mL
¾ teaspoon	4 mL	⅔ cup	150 mL
1 teaspoon	5 mL	¾ cup	175 mL
1 tablespoon	15 mL	1 cup	250 mL
2 tablespoons	25 mL	10 oz. can	285 mL

1 oz. with	25 g		
¼ lb. with	125 g	1 lb. with	500 g
½ lb. with	250 g	1½ lb. with	700 g
¾ lb. with	350 g	2 lb. with	1 kg
			etc. . . .

Initially — round **down** sugar and salt
— if recipe has a lot of flour, ⅔ cup liquid may have to become 175 mL and ¾ cup may have to become 200 mL, to offset the extra flour and prevent a dry product.

Pans, Casseroles

8 x 8	20 x 20 cm, 2L	8 x 2 round, 20 x 5 cm, 2L
9 x 9	22 x 22 cm, 2.5L	9 x 2 round, 22 x 5 cm, 2.5L
9 x 13	22 x 33 cm, 4L	8 x 4 x 3 loaf, 20 x 10 x 7 cm, 1.5L
10 x 15	25 x 38 cm, 4.5L	9 x 5 x 3 loaf, 23 x 12 x 7 cm, 2L

Oven Temperatures

Fahrenheit	Celsius
275°	140°
300°	150°
325°	160°
350°	180°
375°	190°
400°	200°
425°	220°
450°	230°

A special thank you to all who helped test the recipes in this book.

Betty Afaganis
Heather Baker
Ann Black
Charles Bucknor
Charmaine Bucknor
Jim Clark
Margaret Coleman
Garth Cooper
Charles Davies
S. Ditchburn
Jan Dobbins
Brian Duclos
Sheila Elkington
Dick Fusse
Colin Glassco
Karen Grant
Susannah Hamer
Leanne Heron
Bonnie Hewson
Daniele James
Mary Laughren
Coral Luscombe
John Neilson
Richard Nuxoll
Debbie Reibel
Mary-Lou Siemenson
Susan Spoor
Brigid Stewart
Lloyd Sutherland
Ethel Waddell
Robert Walker
Charlotte Williams

Recipe Index

Donor Recipe Index

The Perfect Gift for a Friend

Repas de Deux

Please send _____ copies of
REPAS DE DEUX at $9.95 each, plus $1.50 each for postage and handling to:

Name: _____

Street: _____

City: _____

Province/State: _____ Postal Code/Zip _____

Make cheque or money order payable to:
Repas de Deux
6439 Silver Springs Way
Calgary, Alberta
Canada   T3B 3G1

The Perfect Gift for a Friend

Repas de Deux

Please send _____ copies of
REPAS DE DEUX at $9.95 each, plus $1.50 each for postage and handling to:

Name: _____

Street: _____

City: _____

Province/State: _____ Postal Code/Zip _____

Make cheque or money order payable to:
Repas de Deux
6439 Silver Springs Way
Calgary, Alberta
Canada   T3B 3G1